Portugal Travel Guide

Explore the Country & Speak Portuguese

Like a Local!

3 Books in 1

Explore to Win

THIS COLLECTION INCLUDES THE FOLLOWING BOOKS:

Lisbon Travel Guide

Porto Travel Guide

Algarve Travel Guide

BONUS: Portuguese Phrase Book

Table of Contents

BOOK 4

Portuguese Phrase Book

$100+ FREE BONUSES

Portugal Audio Pronunciations

Portugal Travel Hacking Guide

Portugal Travel Hacks Audiobook

Portugal Visual Travel Guide

Portugal Travel Itineraries

Portugal Budget Travel Guide

Scan QR code to claim your bonuses

— OR —

visit bit.ly/3uGjXE4

BOOK 1

Lisbon Travel Guide

Explore to Win

Introduction

When Portugal pops into conversation, most folks swoop straight to the fancy beaches or pastries they've heard stories about. Sure, pastries are divine (and yes, we'll definitely get into that, don't you worry), but there's a city that truly deserves the spotlight: Lisbon. Now, Lisbon isn't just another European capital. Oh no. It's the cool cousin with a history as deep as the ocean it overlooks, packed with stories just waiting to be discovered.

Now, I get it. You might be worried about missing out on the best spots or perhaps getting lost in the maze of its cobbled streets. Maybe you're anxious about accidentally ordering twelve sardines instead of one at a restaurant because you mixed up your Portuguese numbers (Oddly specific, I know.)

You might be wondering, "Yet another travel guide? Do we really need this?" Oh, trust me, we've heard the murmurs in the alleyways. We're not here just to tell you where to buy the best custard tart. We're diving deep, ensuring you sidestep the touristy trap doors and get a genuine sip of the Lisboa brew. The thing about Lisbon is, that while it's easy to skim the surface, the magic, my friend, is in the details.

This guide? It's your no-nonsense companion. We won't just nudge you to the popular Bairro Alto or Belem. Nope. Prepare to wander off the beaten path, discover local haunts, and even perfect your "obrigado" without sounding like you're ordering a burrito. (Don't fret; we've all been there.)

Now, here's a little secret between us: there's more to Lisbon than its iconic trams and tiled façades. The city's essence is nestled in its people's laughter, in the way old men play cards outside corner cafés, in the hushed tones of fado that fill the night. And guess what? We're committed to helping you find and feel all of that.

I promise, by the time you're done with this guide, you'll not only know how to navigate the city streets, but you'll also find yourself in delightful conversations, sharing stories with the locals and maybe even dancing a spontaneous sardinha dance during one of the city's lively festivals.

There's no sugar-coating here. Yes, there will be uphill walks (Lisbon loves her seven hills), and you might have an occasional misadventure, like taking the tram in the wrong direction (been there, done that!). But that's all part of the journey. It's those unexpected twists and turns, the unplanned detours, that make traveling in Lisbon so magical.

Embracing the essence of Lisbon means getting comfortable with the unexpected, much like the journey I found myself on here. Behind this guide is a lover of stories, someone who, while not Portuguese by birth, has adopted Lisbon as a second home.

Years back, on my first visit, I was merely a wide-eyed tourist, clutching onto my map and carefully planning my day. Fast forward to now, and Lisbon has become my muse, a place where I've laughed, danced, loved, and yes, occasionally lost my way. But in those moments of wandering, I stumbled upon tales and memories that no conventional guide ever mentioned.

My connection with the city isn't just fleeting visits. I've been in those dimly lit Fado bars until the early hours, I've haggled at Feira da Ladra (Lisbon's iconic flea market), and I've penned chapters of my books while sipping espresso at a corner café.

I want to share Lisbon with you the same way a friend would - with all the cherished secrets, those candid moments, and of course, where to find the crispiest Bacalhau.

So, while there's a world of information at your fingertips, know that this guide offers a unique perspective. One crafted not just from meticulous research, but from genuine love and countless sunrises spent wandering Lisbon's streets.

Let's make this journey unforgettable. Grab this guide, and let's uncover the heartbeats and whispers of this enchanting city together. Ready to join me? Onwards!

Chapter 1: Lisbon – The City of Seven Hills

"The beauty of Lisbon is that even though it's increasingly popular with tourists, it's very easy to get off the beaten track."

- Susie Bubble

Lisbon, with its seven hills, is kind of like the workout you never knew you signed up for. You arrive, geared up for sunsets and sangria, and before you know it, you're unintentionally getting the leg workout of a lifetime.

But, hey, who's complaining? Think of it this way: with each uphill battle comes a panoramic reward, and every downhill stroll feels like a carnival slide. Seriously, who needs a gym membership when the city's terrain naturally tones those calves? If Rome boasts seven kings and Snow White has seven dwarves, then Lisbon confidently struts with its seven hills, each whispering tales more intriguing than the last.

Strap on comfy shoes, and let's explore these high-rise wonders together, where every step is a story, and every incline, is an invitation to more mischief and marvels!

A Ride Through Lisbon's Past

Let's time-travel a bit. Imagine a city that has seen it all. From prehistoric settlers to a starry-eyed age of discoveries. From earthquakes that reshaped its streets to revolutions that redefined its spirit. That's Lisbon for you.

Before Christ's Sandals Trod the Earth: Believe it or not, our dear Lisbon has been the cool kid on the block for more than 3,000 years!

Tagus River: Prehistoric tribes chose the banks of the River Tagus to settle. Why? Prime riverfront property with splendid views, obviously!

Roman Rendezvous: Fast forward a bit, and you'd find the Romans setting foot in town around 205 BC.

- **Olisipo:** The old name for Lisbon. Say it three times, and it almost sounds like a spell, doesn't it?
- **Strategic Point:** They weren't here for the pastéis de nata. Olisipo was pivotal in connecting the vast Roman Empire.

Moorish Influence: After the Romans, the Moors made an entrance around the 8th century.

- **Architectural Aesthetics:** You can thank these folks for the city's unique blend of architectural styles.
- **Seven Hills, Not Just a Myth:** The Moors loved a good vantage point; hence, they picked the highest hills to build their neighborhoods.

Fiery Earthquake & Tsunami Tales: 1755. A date the city won't ever forget.

- **Shaken & Stirred:** One of the deadliest earthquakes in history, followed by a massive tsunami and fires, changed Lisbon's landscape forever.
- **Marquês de Pombal:** This chap's resilience post-disaster led to the architectural rebirth of the city.

Golden Age of Discovery:

- **World, Meet Portugal:** From Vasco da Gama to Ferdinand Magellan, Lisbon was the launchpad for many iconic voyages that etched their names in history books.
- **Spice, and Everything Nice:** Thanks to these explorations, Lisbon turned into Europe's first spice market. Cha-ching!

20th Century & Beyond:

- **Revolution of the Carnations:** 1974 saw a nearly bloodless coup that reshaped Portugal's political landscape. And yes, carnations were involved. (Trust Lisbon to keep things stylish.)
- **European Capital of Culture:** In 1994, the world finally acknowledged what we knew all along - Lisbon's undying charm and significance.

Lisbon's journey wasn't always smooth sailing. But like any great story, its highs and lows are what make it so utterly captivating.

Now, when most think of Lisbon's maritime tales, they remember the famous navigators and their grand journeys. But, ah, there's more to the story, hidden beneath the surface.

Golden Age of Discovery: When Lisbon Charted the Unknown

Vasco da Gama

Vasco da Gama. No, he wasn't just a name you had to memorize for a history test back in school. Da Gama was Portugal's star explorer, and his discoveries placed Lisbon on the world's maritime map. Setting sail in 1497, he found the sea route to India, opening up spicy new horizons (literally) for European trade.

Practicalities:

- **Monument to the Discoveries:** Head to the Belem district and marvel at the iconic monument dedicated to Portugal's age of exploration. Da Gama, of course, holds a prime position.
- **Lisbon Maritime Museum:** For those who want a deep dive into da Gama's voyages and maritime history, this museum is a treasure trove.

Local Tip:

Ask any Lisboeta, and they'll tell you about the old tavern in Alfama that celebrates da Gama's spirit with a signature cocktail. It's a blend of spices he brought back from India, combined with local spirits. A sip literally takes you on a journey!

Marquis of Pombal

Now, onto the Marquis of Pombal. If there ever was a man of action, it was him. After the devastating 1755 earthquake, he was the driving force behind Lisbon's rebirth. He designed the Baixa district with its grid-like streets and uniformed buildings, proving disasters can't dampen Lisbon's spirit.

Practicalities:

- **Praça do Marquês de Pombal:** This bustling square, marked by a prominent statue of the Marquis, serves as a reminder of his indomitable spirit.
- **Pombaline Downtown:** A walk through the streets of the Baixa district gives you a glimpse of his vision—a phoenix's rise from the ashes.

Local Tip:

In Baixa, find the lesser-known café with vintage tiles depicting Pombal's reconstruction efforts. Not only will you get a history lesson, but the pastries are to die for! They have a special cinnamon twist, said to be Marquis's favorite. So, indulge in a treat while soaking in a bit of history.

Lisbon's Local Customs and Etiquettes: A Traveler's Quick Guide

- **Greetings Matter:** When meeting someone for the first time, a handshake accompanied by direct eye contact is standard. Among friends, it's common to exchange two-cheek kisses (starting with the right).
  - **Tip:** Don't rush the greeting. A little warmth goes a long way.

- **Casual Yet Respectful:** Lisboetas are generally informal and friendly. However, addressing elders or strangers? It's best to use formal titles until invited otherwise.

- **Table Manners:** Wait for the host to start before digging in. If you're at a local's home, it's polite to finish everything on your plate.
  - **Tip:** If you're enjoying the meal (and why wouldn't you?), a hearty "Está delicioso!" (It's delicious!) will always be appreciated.

- **Tipping:** It's customary to leave a 10% tip at restaurants. However, always check the bill, as some establishments already include a service charge.

- **Quiet Please:** While Lisbon is lively, it's polite to keep noise levels down, especially during the late evening and early morning in residential areas.

- **Public Transport:** Give up your seat for elderly passengers, pregnant women, or parents with small children on trams and buses.

- **Sunday Observance:** Sunday remains a family day, and many shops are closed. Respect the local customs and plan your shopping on other days.
  - **Tip:** This is an excellent day for beach lounging or a scenic tram ride.

- **Speak Softly:** Portuguese people usually speak at a moderate volume in public places. Loud conversations, especially in enclosed spaces like restaurants or public transport, might be perceived as rude.

- **Touristy Things Are A-OK!:** Here's the thing. While it's awesome to blend in and adopt local customs, you're a traveler, and there's no shame in that. Want to hop on that super touristy tram for a classic Lisbon photo? Go for it!
  - o **Controversial Tip:** Embrace your tourist status. Sure, try to respect local customs and immerse yourself. But don't feel bad about wanting to do the iconic (and yes, sometimes clichéd) things. That's part of the travel experience too!
- **Mind Your Attire:** Lisbon is quite laid-back, but if you're visiting religious sites, it's respectful to cover your shoulders and avoid shorts or skimpy dresses.

Seasonal Festivals and Celebrations in Lisbon

- **Carnaval (February/March)**
  - o *What:* Think of it as Portugal's version of Mardi Gras. Though it's celebrated across the country, Lisbon has its own colorful parades, dances, and costume parties.
  - o *Highlight:* Join in the revelry with masks and get ready for some traditional Carnaval songs!

- **Peixe em Lisboa - Lisbon Fish & Flavors (April)**
  - o *What:* A food festival that celebrates the city's rich seafood heritage.
  - o *Highlight:* Taste some of the best seafood dishes from renowned chefs and local eateries.

- **Dia de Liberdade - Freedom Day (April 25)**

- *What:* A national holiday that commemorates the Carnation Revolution of 1974, which ended decades of dictatorship.
- *Highlight*: Witness the marches, concerts, and commemorative events throughout the city.

- **Festas de Lisboa (June)**
  - *What:* A month-long celebration with street parties, parades, and music.
  - *Highlight:* The lively celebrations for Santo António, Lisbon's patron saint, on June 12th and 13th. Don't miss the traditional parade along Avenida da Liberdade.

- **Fado Festival (September)**
  - *What:* Celebrates Fado, Portugal's soulful traditional music recognized as a UNESCO World Heritage treasure.
  - *Highlight:* Intimate Fado performances in some of the city's historic neighborhoods.

- **DocLisboa (October)**
  - *What:* Lisbon's international documentary film festival showcasing a broad range of films from across the globe.
  - *Highlight:* Screenings are held in iconic venues, including the Culturgest and the Cinema São Jorge.

- **Lisbon & Sintra Film Festival (November)**
  - *What:* An event that attracts cinephiles and top international filmmakers.
  - *Highlight:* Besides film screenings, there are also art exhibitions, concerts, and masterclasses.

- **Natal (December)**

- o *What:* The festive Christmas season lights up Lisbon with decorations, markets, and activities.
- o *Highlight:* Wander through the city's squares like Rossio and Praça do Comércio, which are illuminated and bustling with festive vibes.

- **Passagem de Ano - New Year's Eve (December 31)**
  - o *What:* Welcoming the New Year with grand celebrations.
  - o *Highlight:* The fireworks display over the river Tagus, best enjoyed along the waterfront.

Lisbon's vibrant festivities offer an immersive cultural experience, allowing visitors to feel the city's heartbeat. If you can, plan your trip around these celebrations to truly see Lisbon in all its radiant splendor!

Key Takeaways

- **Lisbon's Unique Landscape:** Nestled on seven hills, Lisbon offers panoramic vistas at every turn. The city's undulating terrain adds to its charm and provides numerous viewpoints for breathtaking scenery.
- **Historical Richness:** From Phoenicians and Moors to its Age of Discoveries with figures like Vasco da Gama, Lisbon has a tapestry of histories woven into its streets, making it a living museum of varied pasts.
- **Local Etiquette Matters:** While Lisboetas are welcoming, it's always good to familiarize yourself with local customs. Whether it's how to greet or the appropriate behavior in religious places, being mindful of these can enhance your experience.
- **Be a Tourist, Embrace It:** It's okay to indulge in touristy activities. After all, they're popular for a reason! Sightseeing trams, Fado houses, and those famous custard tarts are all worth the experience.
- **Vibrant Festivals:** Lisbon is alive with celebrations throughout the year. From the colorful Carnival to the soulful Fado Festival, there's always something happening in the city that adds an extra layer of cultural immersion to your visit.
- **Deep Dive, Not Just Skim:** To truly appreciate Lisbon, you must delve deeper. Beyond the iconic landmarks lie stories, traditions, and local hangouts that give you a genuine feel of the city's heart and soul.

Action Steps

- **Map It Out:** Grab a city map and mark the seven hills of Lisbon. Plan a route that takes you to at least one viewpoint from each hill, ensuring you get panoramic views from different angles.

- **Historical Exploration:** Dedicate a day to trace the city's historical timeline. Start with a visit to the Alfama district, Lisbon's oldest neighborhood, and gradually move to more recent landmarks.
- **Try Local Delicacies:** Make a list of local dishes and snacks you want to try. Seek out the best spots for each, be it the famed pastel de nata or the savory bacalhau.
- **Respect and Integrate Local Customs:** Now that you're aware of the local etiquette, practice them daily. A simple "obrigado" or "obrigada" (thank you) can go a long way in building connections.
- **Book a Tour:** Even if it feels too "touristy", book at least one guided tour. Whether it's a tram tour, a Fado show, or a walking tour, this is a great way to get curated insights about the city.
- **Attend a Local Festival:** Check out the city's event calendar and see if there are any local festivals or events happening during your visit. It's a brilliant way to immerse yourself in local culture.
- **Journal Your Experience:** At the end of each day, jot down your experiences, conversations, and any interesting tidbits you've learned. This not only helps in processing the day but also serves as a fantastic keepsake.
- **Engage with Locals:** Don't shy away from starting conversations. Whether it's a café owner, a fellow tram passenger, or a street performer, engage in light conversations. You'll be surprised at the stories and tips you might gather!
- **Step Out of Your Comfort Zone:** Try something new every day. It could be tasting a dish you've never heard of, exploring a neighborhood on a whim, or even joining a local dance!

Chapter 2: Must-Visit Sites in Lisbon

"Oh salty sea, how much of your salt is tears from Portugal?"

– Fernando Pessoa

My grandma always used to say, 'The best views come after the hardest climbs.' Boy, did Lisbon put that to the test. I finally understood what she meant the moment I set foot on its cobblestoned hills and caught sight of the azure Tagus River winking back at me. But let's not get swept away just yet. Lisbon isn't only about steep walks and postcard vistas; it's also a treasure trove of places that'll make you go 'Whoa, I gotta Instagram this!' Strap in; we're going on a tour of sites that'll tickle your wanderlust and make your grandma's wise words echo in your head.

Belem Tower

Let's step into a time capsule. Because Belem Tower is not just another brick in the wall; it's a 500-year-old chess piece overlooking the Tagus River. This UNESCO World Heritage Site has witnessed the ebb and flow of explorers and empires, and my friend, it's high time you and I sailed those historical waters.

Why It's Noteworthy

- **Architectural Marvel:** With its Manueline style, the tower is like a lesson in Portuguese history, except instead of dozing off, you're wide awake taking selfies.

- **Historical Significance:** Built in the early 16th century, it's seen everyone from explorers setting off to conquer new worlds to local fishermen conquering, well, fish.
- **Strategic Location:** Originally situated in the middle of the Tagus River, the tower served as both a fortress and a ceremonial gateway.

Practical Information

- **Getting There:** Take tram 15 or 127 from the city center to Belém. It's a 30-minute ride.
- **Time to Spend:** At least 2-3 hours if you really want to soak it in.
- **Entrance Fee:** €6 for adults, with various discounts available.
- **Hours:** 10 am to 5:30 pm, closed on Mondays.

Local Tips and Tricks

- **Skip the Lines:** Tickets can be pre-purchased online. Seriously, don't wait in line like a rookie.
- **Photography:** The best photos are taken from the pier just opposite the tower, especially during sunset.
- **Footwear:** Cobblestone alert! Leave the heels at the hotel and opt for comfortable shoes.

Budget Tips

- **Combo Tickets:** Consider getting a combo ticket if you're also planning to visit Jerónimos Monastery. It's a win-win.
- **Free Sundays:** If you're an early bird and an EU resident, entrance is free on Sundays until 2 pm.

Don't Just Stand There

Now that you've soaked in all that history, take a moment. Lean against the sturdy walls that have stood the test of time. Imagine the fleets of ships that passed by, their sails full of dreams and dread. Then snap back to reality, and maybe get yourself one of those iconic pastéis de nata from nearby Pastéis de Belém.

Jerónimos Monastery

Step into the Jerónimos Monastery, and you'll feel like you've walked into an opulent episode of 'Portugal's Got History.' Trust me; you don't want to miss this one. This grand structure, a masterpiece of Manueline architecture, is where Vasco da Gama spent his last night before heading off to navigate a sea route to India. No big deal, right?

Why You Must Visit

Beyond its architectural grandeur, the monastery is a symbol of Portugal's Age of Discovery. It's not just about oohs and aahs over the intricate arches. The place packs in history, with tombs of legendary figures like Vasco da Gama and poet Luís de Camões.

Best Time to Visit

The sweet spots for avoiding the dreaded 'tourist shoulder bump' are from March to May and September to October. Lisbon shows off its radiant self during these months, and the monastery is no exception.

Insider Tips

- **Book Tickets in Advance:** This isn't your hidden corner café; it's one of Portugal's most visited spots. Skip the queue and buy tickets online. Some offers even bundle it with other nearby attractions.

- **Footwear is Key:** You'll be pacing through history, quite literally. Slip into some comfortable shoes; your feet will thank you.
- **Dress Code:** It's a monastery, folks. Bring out your modest gear; let's keep the skin-show for the beach.
- **Timings:** Aim for a window between 12 pm and 2 pm. Most tour buses roll in either before or after this period, giving you some space to breathe and snap those unobstructed photos.
- **Combo Deals:** Look for ticket options that pair a visit here with other Belem jewels like the Belem Tower. Two birds, one stone.
- **Nearby Attractions:** You're in Belem, a district brimming with must-sees. Don't just bolt after the monastery. The Belem Tower and the Monument to the Discoveries are within walking distance.

Handy Information

- **Location:** Praça do Império 1400-206 Lisboa, Portugal
- **Opening Hours:** 10 am - 5:30 pm (winter) and 10 am - 6:30 pm (summer)
- **Ticket Price:** €10 for adults, discounts available for students and seniors. Free on the first Sunday of each month.
- **Time to Spend:** Expect to spend 2-3 hours for a thorough visit.
- **Public Transport:** Take tram 15 or bus number 728 to get to Belem. The monastery is a 5-minute walk from the station.
- **Parking:** Limited street parking is available but filling up fast; consider public transport.
- **Accessibility:** Wheelchair accessible with facilities for differently-abled visitors.
- **Facilities:** Restrooms, gift shops, and small cafes are available on site.
- **Language:** Most signage and tours are available in English.

Remember, Lisbon waits for no one, but Jerónimos Monastery might just make you want to slow down and soak it all in. Be smart, plan ahead, and this historic jewel will give you stories worth their weight in golden maritime history.

Alfama District

Alfama is the oldest district in Lisbon and a living museum of the city's Moorish past. Think winding streets, surprise viewpoints, and the soulful sound of Fado drifting through the air. You haven't truly experienced Lisbon until you've got lost in Alfama's labyrinth.

Best Time to Visit

Evenings are enchanting due to the Fado performances, but daytime visits are equally charming with fewer crowds. June is especially festive because of the Santo António Festival. The cooler months of March to May and September to October offer a more comfortable experience.

Handy Information

- **Location:** East of the city center, spreading from the São Jorge Castle down to the River Tagus.
- **Opening Hours:** Always open, but individual shops and venues have their own hours.
- **Ticket Price:** Free to wander, but attractions like the São Jorge Castle have an entry fee.
- **Time to Spend:** At least half a day, if not a full one.
- **Public Transport:** Tram 28 stops at various points in Alfama. Alternatively, take the metro to Santa Apolónia station.
- **Parking:** Highly limited. Alfama is best explored on foot anyway.

- **Facilities:** Numerous Fado bars, cafes, souvenir shops, and historical points of interest.

Insider Tips

- **Walking Tour:** Consider joining a walking tour to get the historical background of the area.
- **Fado:** Alfama is the birthplace of Fado, so don't skip on visiting a Fado bar for a soul-stirring performance.
- **Miradouros:** Don't miss the viewpoints like Miradouro das Portas do Sol and Miradouro de Santa Luzia for Instagram-worthy shots.
- **Safety:** Generally safe but like any touristy area, keep an eye on your belongings.
- **Footwear:** Cobbled streets are charming but can be tricky. Wear comfy, anti-slip shoes.

Pair Alfama with a visit to the São Jorge Castle for a day steeped in history, culture, and spectacular views. It's the essence of Lisbon in one charming package, so make the most of it!

Baixa District

In contrast to Alfama's ancient charm, Baixa is the neoclassical face of Lisbon, rebuilt after the 1755 earthquake. Think grand squares, symmetrical streets, and a plethora of shops and eateries. A stroll through Baixa is like a walk through a European postcard, only better because you're actually there.

Best Time to Visit

Spring and fall offer milder weather and fewer crowds. During the evenings, the district lights up, offering a different yet equally captivating experience.

Handy Information

- **Location:** Central Lisbon, nestled between Alfama and Chiado.
- **Opening Hours:** Shops typically operate from 9 AM - 8 PM; dining spots may remain open later.
- **Ticket Price:** No entry fee for the district itself.
- **Time to Spend:** 2-4 hours will suffice for a basic tour, but you could easily spend a whole day.
- **Public Transport:** Metro stations Baixa-Chiado and Rossio are conveniently located.
- **Parking:** Limited. Public transport is a better option.
- **Facilities:** Upscale shops, traditional cafes, historic attractions, and excellent dining options.

Insider Tips

- **Elevador de Santa Justa:** Don't miss this 19th-century lift offering panoramic views of the city.
- **Pastéis de Nata:** Pop into any bakery to try this iconic Portuguese pastry.
- **Praça do Comércio:** This square is a perfect place for photos and people-watching.
- **Rossio Square:** A bustling spot with a wavy-patterned pavement that's a marvel in itself.
- **Wine and Dine:** From swanky restaurants to vintage cafés, Baixa has a range of options to cater to all tastes and budgets.

Bairro Alto

Why You Must Visit

If Baixa is the elegant face of Lisbon, Bairro Alto is its untamed soul. By day, it's a quiet, almost sleepy neighborhood. But as dusk falls, the area comes alive with Fado music, spirited bars, and artistic flair. It's the kind of place where you're as likely to stumble upon a cutting-edge art gallery as you are a 100-year-old tavern.

Best Time to Visit

For daytime exploration, weekdays are quieter. For nightlife, weekends are your best bet. Note that many businesses in Bairro Alto are closed on Sundays.

Handy Information

- **Location:** West of Baixa and Chiado.
- **Opening Hours:** Varied by establishment, many open late into the night.
- **Ticket Price:** Free to roam.
- **Time to Spend:** At least half a day to get a real sense of its dual personality.
- **Public Transport:** Baixa-Chiado metro station is about a 10-minute walk.
- **Parking:** Challenging, especially during weekends.
- **Facilities:** Numerous bars, clubs, boutiques, and restaurants.

Insider Tips

- **Experience Fado:** Try Tasca do Chico for a memorable Fado experience. Arrive early to grab a seat.
- **Street Art:** Keep an eye out for murals and graffiti that showcase local talent.
- **Miradouro de São Pedro de Alcântara:** This viewpoint offers a magnificent cityscape, especially during sunset.
- **Bar Hopping:** The nightlife here is unlike any other part of the city, featuring anything from wine bars to underground clubs.
- **Tram 28:** This iconic tram line passes close by, providing an alternate and charming mode of transport.

St. George's Castle

Perched atop the highest hill in Lisbon, St. George's Castle (Castelo de São Jorge) stands as a sentinel overlooking the city and the Tagus River beyond. Its sturdy walls and towers have witnessed over a millennium of history, from its initial days as a Moorish fortress in the 11th century to its role as a royal residence during Portugal's Age of Discovery.

The castle complex includes not only the military fortification but also gardens, viewpoints, and archaeological exhibits. It serves as both a historical site and an urban oasis, offering spectacular panoramic views that make you feel like you're looking at a postcard.

Why You Must Visit

St. George's Castle offers jaw-dropping panoramic views of the city. Explore ramparts, walk through ancient ruins, and get lost in time as you step into this centuries-old fortress.

Best Time to Visit

Early morning or late afternoon are ideal to avoid crowds and the heat. The castle is busiest during the summer months, from May to August.

Handy Information

- **Location:** Castle Hill, Alfama district.
- **Opening Hours:** 9 am – 9 pm (Mar-Oct), 9 am – 6 pm (Nov-Feb).
- **Ticket Price:** €10 for adults, €5 for kids. Free admission for residents.
- **Time to Spend:** 2–3 hours.
- **Public Transport:** Bus 737 from Praça da Figueira or take tram 28 to Miradouro Santa Luzia and walk.

- **Parking:** Limited, best to go by public transport.
- **Facilities:** Café, gift shop, and restrooms available on site.

Insider Tips

- **Camera Obscura:** Don't miss the periscope view of the city, located in the Tower of Ulysses.
- **Guided Tours:** Consider a guided tour to delve into the castle's rich history.
- **Footwear:** Wear sturdy shoes. The cobblestones and slopes are not stiletto-friendly.
- **Picnic:** There are spots within the castle grounds for a perfect picnic with a view.
- **Combo Tickets:** You can often get a combo ticket that includes other nearby attractions like the Lisbon Cathedral.

Mouraria

Mouraria is one of Lisbon's oldest districts, its history tracing back to medieval times. The name "Mouraria" literally translates to "Moorish quarter," as this was the area where the Moors were allowed to live after the Christian Reconquest of Lisbon in 1147. Over the centuries, it has evolved into a cultural melting pot, showcasing an amalgamation of influences from Africa, Asia, and the Middle East.

Today, it's a neighborhood where tradition and modernity coexist. Ancient houses with tiles (azulejos) stand next to modern boutiques and art studios. You'll find churches sharing streets with mosques and temples, embodying the spirit of coexistence that defines Lisbon. With its narrow alleys, hidden courtyards, and numerous cultural spots, Mouraria is a living, breathing museum of Lisbon's diverse history and present-day inclusivity.

Why You Must Visit

Mouraria, often overshadowed by Alfama, is where Lisbon's soul resides. From the birthplace of Fado music to streets pulsating with multi-ethnic vibes, Mouraria offers an authentic Lisbon experience that's impossible to forget.

Best Time to Visit

Evening is the perfect time to visit Mouraria. The Fado bars come to life, and the neighborhood is bathed in the soft glow of street lamps and storefronts.

Handy Information

- **Location:** East of the city center, adjacent to Alfama.
- **Time to Spend:** 3–4 hours or an entire evening.
- **Public Transport:** Metro (Martim Moniz or Intendente station), tram 28, or a 15-minute walk from Baixa.
- **Facilities:** Plenty of Fado bars, restaurants, shops, and cafes.

Insider Tips

- **Listen to Fado:** Visit Maria da Mouraria, a historical Fado house.
- **Street Art:** Keep an eye out for stunning street murals around the district.
- **Eat Well:** Try a dish at a Cape Verdean or Goan restaurant.
- **Walking Tour:** Consider a guided walking tour to explore hidden corners.
- **Safety:** The area is generally safe, but like any city district, stay alert.

Budget Tips

- Fado performances can sometimes be free if you dine at the bar or restaurant.
- Street food options are both delicious and budget-friendly.

Rua Augusta Arch

Lisbon is a city of layers, each one revealing a different tale of time, and the Rua Augusta Arch is a grand bookmark in its storied history. Originally conceptualized to commemorate the city's reconstruction after the devastating earthquake of 1755, today the arch stands as a symbol of resilience.

Why You Must Visit

Look, we all know the Rua Augusta Arch is Insta-gold, but let me tell you, your feet's going to thank you for the killer 360-degree views from the rooftop terrace. I mean, where else can you capture the sparkling Tagus River, the ancient St. George's Castle, and the city's rolling hills all in one frame? Trust me, your followers are gonna eat this up.

Best Time to Visit

To avoid crowds and bask in the morning light, aim for an early visit around 9–10 a.m. Sunsets here are divine but be prepared for it to be busier.

Handy Information

- **Location:** Praça do Comércio, Baixa.
- **Time to Spend:** About 1 hour.
- **Entrance Fee:** Approximately €3 for adults.
- **Public Transport:** Metro (Terreiro do Paço station), tram 15 or 25, bus routes 206, 207, 208.

- **Facilities:** Small museum inside the arch, rooftop viewing area.

Insider Tips
- **Buy Tickets Online:** You can often skip the line by pre-booking.
- **Footwear:** Wear comfortable shoes. The climb, although not too strenuous, requires ease of movement.
- **Photography:** Take a zoom lens for detailed shots of the sculptures and sophisticated details.

Budget Tips
- Save by bundling your ticket with other attractions in the area.

LX Factory

You know how everyone thinks Europe is all about castles and cobblestones? Well, LX Factory slams that notion like a headliner at a rock concert. This place is where Lisbon's edgy soul jams out loud. It's under the Ponte 25 de Abril bridge—a location as unexpected as finding an underground club in your grandma's basement.

With graffiti that belongs in modern art museums and cafes that double as art installations, LX Factory will make you rethink what Europe—and Lisbon—is all about. Trust me, it's the chill backyard party you didn't know Lisbon had, and you're on the VIP list.

Why You Must Visit

You wouldn't miss the final season of your favorite show, would you? Well, skipping LX Factory feels a lot like that—a total cliffhanger in your Lisbon saga. This place is where the city lets its hair down and tosses the rulebook. Forget what you think you know about Lisbon; LX Factory is the B-side track that steals the show. Trust me, you'll leave with more than a keepsake; you'll have a brand new playlist for life.

Best Time to Visit

Weekend afternoons are bustling, filled with live music and local markets. But if you're the type who likes to wander without the crowd, a weekday morning offers a more serene experience.

Insider Tips

- Hit up "Ler Devagar," a bookstore that's basically the lovechild of a bibliophile and a steampunk architect.
- Feeling peckish? "Mez Cais LX" has mouthwatering mezze that pairs perfectly with the casual, artsy vibe.
- Don't forget to check out the rooftop of "Rio Maravilha" for a cocktail and a view of the bridge that'll make your Instagram scream #NoFilterNeeded.

Hidden Gems of Lisbon

Welcome to the Lisbon you didn't know you needed. Forget the travel blogs and their mainstream haunts; we're about to take a detour into the city's best-kept secrets. Buckle up!

The Doll Hospital (Hospital de Bonecas)

If you ever wondered where Hello Kitty goes to recover after one too many adventures, it's probably the Doll Hospital (Hospital de Bonecas) in Lisbon. No joke, this place is the ER for dolls—and not just any dolls, but generations of dolls! We're talking antique figurines, Barbie's less famous cousins, and even your childhood teddy who's seen better days.

Why You Must Visit:

Now, you might be thinking, "Why would I want to go to a doll hospital?" Let me tell you, stepping into this peculiar spot is like strolling through the pages of a fantasy novel. It's not just for fixing up your old toys; it's a living museum where you can see dolls from every era getting a "facelift." You'll leave contemplating the life cycles of inanimate objects; it's that deep.

Best Time to Visit:

Anytime you're in need of an offbeat experience or soulful reflection, this doll haven will do the trick. They're open Monday through Saturday, so pick your day and plunge into the uncanny valley.

Insider Tips:

- The place can get busy, especially on weekends, so if you're looking for a quieter experience, shoot for a weekday visit.
- Don't forget to check out their historical exhibit. It's a mini timeline of doll evolution, minus the Darwinism.

Jardim do Torel

Jardim do Torel is the place where even Romeo and Juliet would put their family feud on pause to snap a selfie. Seriously, this garden is the epitome of romance meets urban sanctuary. Nestled atop a hill, it's where lovebirds and lone wolves alike come for that much-needed escape.

Why You Must Visit:

Besides its panoramic city views, Jardim do Torel offers a unique combo of vintage charm and modern quirks. Think classic statues interspersed with contemporary art installations. It's like a never-ending first date with Lisbon—you discover something new and endearing every time you visit. Plus, there's a bar that turns into a beach in the summer. Yes, you read that right, a sandy beach with umbrellas and all!

Best Time to Visit:

Late afternoon or early evening. This is when the light plays tricks with the skyline and transforms the garden into a canvas of golden hues. Perfect for those who fancy themselves photographers—or just need to update their dating profile pic.

Insider Tips:

- If you're up for a small hike, take the stairs; otherwise, the Elevador do Lavra will get you to this hilltop haven without the sweat.
- The garden hosts events, like mini-concerts and flea markets. Check their schedule and plan your visit around it for an extra layer of awesomeness.

Conserveira de Lisboa

Conserveira de Lisboa is to canned fish what the food machine in "Cloudy with a Chance of Meatballs" is to, well, meatballs. It's a cornucopia of seafood wonders, housed in a space that screams vintage Portuguese flair.

Why You Must Visit:

Ever thought a can of fish could be high art? Well, Conserveira de Lisboa turns that idea into a reality. Picture aisles brimming with neatly stacked tins, each adorned with labels that look like they were designed by Picasso during his marine life phase. If you're a foodie or just appreciate the weirder, kitschier side of life, this place is a can't-miss.

Best Time to Visit:

Weekday afternoons. The shop gets swamped during weekends and holidays. Trust me, you don't want to be elbowing your way through a crowd just to get your hands on some premium sardines.

- Ask for a tasting! You'll want to know the difference between a spiced mackerel and a tuna belly.
- These tinned delicacies make for unique souvenirs or gifts. Who needs another magnet or keychain when you can have artisanal seafood?

Pavilhão Chinês

Alright, if "Narnia" had a boozy older cousin, it'd be Pavilhão Chinês. The moment you step through the door, it's like tumbling into the wardrobe, minus the snow and talking animals—though after a few drinks, who knows?

Why You Must Visit:

This isn't just a bar; it's a fever dream. Think intricate woodwork, five rooms filled with curiosities that would make a pirate blush, and a cocktail list longer than a Tolstoy novel. Whether you're a fan of retro games, military memorabilia, or just kicking back with a drink that has more ingredients than you can pronounce, Pavilhão Chinês is your jam.

Best Time to Visit:

- Post-dinner hours during weekdays for the full experience without the weekend hustle.

Insider Tips:

- If you're a fan of gin, ask for their signature gin and tonic. It's an art form here.
- You'll want to allocate time to roam. Each room has its own vibe, and you don't want to miss the quirky details.
- Despite its elaborate décor, the dress code is casual. But hey, if you want to don your pirate hat or military jacket to blend in with the surroundings, who am I to stop you?

Navigating Through Lisbon's Iconic Tram Routes

Listen up, because we're switching gears, or should I say tracks? You can't really say you've conquered Lisbon until you've lived the tram life. These yellow chariots aren't just a mode of transport; they're as iconic to Lisbon as John Lennon's round glasses are to him. So, let's board this magical mystery tour and find out why Lisbon's trams are the unsung heroes of city travel.

Why Trams Are Your New Best Friends

You could walk, you could Uber, but why? The trams are where you'll share elbow space with grandma toting a grocery bag full of fresh fish, overhear tourists mispronouncing Portuguese street names, and—if you're lucky—catch a live Fado performance by a tram driver who's feeling particularly melodious. Plus, with routes that go uphill, these bad boys save your legs from turning into jelly.

A Quick Tram Route Rundown

- **Tram 28:** This is the Beyoncé of trams. It's the star everyone wants to see. From Graça to Estrela, it covers almost all must-visit spots.
- **Tram 12:** The Ringo Starr of the tram world. It's a circular route around the city center.
- **Tram 15:** Think of this as the Adele of trams, taking you from downtown all the way to Belém.
- **Tram 18 and 25:** The indie artists of tram routes. Not as popular but underrated gems you must experience.

Must-Have Tram Apps

- **Lisboa Move-me:** Real-time updates? Yes, please!
- **Tram Hunter:** Just for fun, it makes you feel like a James Bond on a mission.

Best Time to Board

Avoid rush hours unless you enjoy being a sardine packed in a tin can. Mid-morning or late afternoon is your golden ticket.

Insider Tips

- Buy the Viva Viagem Card. It's the Swiss army knife of Lisbon public transport.
- Always validate your ticket; ticket controllers can appear out of nowhere like Hogwarts professors.
- Keep an eye out for pickpockets; they love the trams as much as you will.

The Costs: Keep Your Wallet Happy

- Single Ticket: €3
- 24-Hour Ticket: €6.40
- Viva Viagem Card: €0.50 (rechargeable)

The "Only in Lisbon" Tram Experiences

- **Sunset Ride on Tram 28:** As the sun sets, the city turns golden, and so does the tram—well, metaphorically.
- **Tram 15 to Belém:** Get your pastéis de nata first, then hop on Tram 15 for a joyride.

The Tram-etiquette

- Give up your seat for those who need it more.
- Don't be the obnoxious tourist blocking the exit.
- Remember, a simple "obrigado" to your tram driver goes a long way.

Bonus Round: Lesser-Known Facts

- Did you know Tram 28 is sometimes called "The Tourist Tram"? Locals avoid it like a vegetarian avoids a steakhouse.

Alright, I've armed you with all you need to know to navigate Lisbon's iconic trams like a seasoned rockstar. Don't be a Yellow Submarine wannabe, be the Yellow Submarine. Hop on, validate that ticket, and make the city your stage.

Key Takeaways

- A must-visit for anyone interested in history and breathtaking views at Belém Tower.
- Visit Jerónimos Monastery between 12 pm and 2 pm for a quieter experience.
- Get lost in the labyrinthine streets of Alfama District for a touch of old Lisbon.
- Early mornings at St. George's Castle offer the best views and fewer crowds.
- Rua Augusta Arch offers panoramic views that redefine Lisbon for you.
- The Doll Hospital is an off-beat gem that's as weird as it is wonderful.
- Jardim do Torel is Lisbon's answer to Romeo and Juliet's balcony.
- Conserveira de Lisboa is an experience as whimsical as a scene from "Cloudy with a Chance of Meatballs."
- Pavilhão Chinês is where a drink serves you stories from multiple eras.
- Tram 28 isn't just a ride; it's an experience.
- Viva Viagem Card is your golden ticket to navigating the city like a local.
- Expect to spend €5 to €20 on entry fees for most attractions.
- Always opt for online tickets to save time.

Action Steps

- Get the Lisboa Card for unlimited public transport and discounted entry to attractions.
- For a true taste of local cuisine, skip the tourist traps and ask a local where they eat. Trust me, your taste buds will thank you.

- Instead of snapping pics of Belém Tower from the shore, rent a kayak to see it from the water. You get a unique angle and an arm workout!
- If you're going to Jerónimos Monastery, aim for weekday visits, and go when they first open or an hour before they close. This is when the lighting is just magical.
- Love Alfama? Do it justice by walking its streets on a Tuesday or Saturday, coinciding with the Feira da Ladra flea market.
- At St. George's Castle, there's a wine cart near the entrance. Buy a glass and savor it as you watch the sun dip below the horizon.
- Want a pic from Rua Augusta Arch without the crowd? Go up just before it closes. The staff doesn't rush you out.
- On your LX Factory visit, make sure to spot the 'Ler Devagar' bookstore. Buy a book by a local author, grab a coffee, and you've got yourself a perfect afternoon.
- When visiting the Doll Hospital, leave room in your schedule to wander the surrounding streets. You'll find a host of boutiques you'd never see otherwise.
- Ditch the tourist trams. For an authentic experience, catch tram 15 or 18, where locals go about their day-to-day.

Take these steps to heart, and you'll be living the Lisboeta life in no time. Hungry for more? I bet you are! Your Lisbon experience would be incomplete without diving into its culinary delights. Trust me, your taste buds are in for a rollercoaster ride. Buckle up and turn the page because the next chapter is all about Lisbon's food scene—from scrumptious pastries to mouth-watering seafood. Let's eat our way through Lisbon, shall we?

Chapter 3: Culinary Journey Through Lisbon

"I've got two places I like to be. Portugal is one"

- Cliff Richard

Before you even think about Googling "What to eat in Lisbon," stop right there! Imagine you're Anthony Bourdain, traveling the world, and you've just landed in Lisbon—this chapter is your Parts Unknown, but way less grim. You're about to unravel the tapestry of Lisbon's culinary landscape, and I guarantee, it's more addictive than your mom's mac 'n' cheese. So, loosen your belt, and let's embark on a foodie pilgrimage that'll make you want to write sonnets about sardines and ballads about bacalhau. Ready to dig in?

The History and Flavors of the Renowned Pastéis de Nata

Hold your horses before you dive into a random bakery to snag one of these custard delights. Let's take a brief detour through the nostalgic and aromatic alleys of Pastéis de Nata's history and flavor profile.

History:

Born in the heart of Lisbon's monasteries, Pastéis de Nata was a recipe devised by monks. Fast forward a couple of centuries, and this humble pastry has turned into a global phenomenon. It's like the Madonna of the pastry world—timeless, versatile, and universally loved.

Flavors:

Now, we're not just talking about custard and puff pastry here. The layers of flavors reveal themselves like the final act of a Shakespearean drama. The custard has a hint of vanilla and cinnamon, and the pastry is so flaky it could probably host a talk show about crumbling relationships.

Variants:

Today, you'll find varieties that include chocolate chips, strawberries, and even exotic spices. While the classic version remains unbeatable, these creative takes are like remixes of your favorite old song— different but still a hit.

Where to Get the Best:

We could argue all day about where to find the best Pastéis de Nata, but let's cut to the chase. If you're in Lisbon, Pastéis de Belém is the OG, the granddaddy of them all. For a modern twist, head over to Manteigaria.

How to Eat:

No, you don't just shove it in your mouth. You take a moment. Sprinkle some powdered sugar and cinnamon on top and take that first bite as if you're tasting love for the first time. Ah, pure bliss!

Making Your Own:

If you're smitten enough to take the relationship to the next level, there are workshops and cooking classes in Lisbon that can help you recreate the magic in your own kitchen. Not saying you'll become a Pastéis de Nata wizard overnight, but hey, Harry Potter wasn't built in a day either.

Bacalhau à Brás

Bacalhau à Brás is the "Chris Hemsworth" of Portuguese dishes—undeniably attractive and utterly charming in a humble, laid-back kinda way. What's it made of? It's a blend of shredded codfish, golden straw fries, and scrambled eggs, all married together with finely chopped parsley and sometimes topped with black olives. Basically, it's comfort food that got a PhD in Deliciousness.

Good to Know:

Here's where things get quirky. Bacalhau à Brás was probably named after its creator, a tavern owner in the Bairro Alto district of Lisbon. But some argue it could be a tribute to the Braz brothers, famous 19th-century cod traders. Who's to say? The point is, the dish is legendary, and its history just adds to its allure.

Best Places to Eat:

If you're looking for the "Rolls Royce" of Bacalhau à Brás, head to "O Ramiro." Yeah, it's mostly known for seafood, but their Bacalhau à Brás is the stuff of legends. Another go-to spot is "A Casa do Bacalhau," which is like a temple for codfish lovers.

When to Eat:

While it's a year-round treat, Bacalhau à Brás is often enjoyed during festivities like Christmas. However, any evening in Lisbon is a good enough reason to indulge.

Alternatives:

So, let's say you're not a cod fan (who are you?!). There's also "Atum à Brás," where the cod is replaced by tuna. It's like the understudy that's waiting in the wings, and it's pretty darn good too.

Pastéis de Nata

Pastéis de Nata is the Portuguese answer to sweet cravings. Picture a flaky, buttery pastry shell filled with creamy custard, and topped off with a dusting of cinnamon and powdered sugar. These little guys are the epitome of simple yet satisfying.

Good to Know:

They originated in the Jerónimos Monastery in Lisbon. These days, you'll find them in every bakery, but not all are created equal.

Best Places to Eat:

Go to "Pastéis de Belém," where it all began. The line might be long, but trust me, it's worth the wait. "Manteigaria" is another top spot, especially if you enjoy watching the baking process.

When to Eat:

Great any time, but they're especially popular in the mornings with a coffee or as an afternoon pick-me-up.

Alternatives:

For something a bit different, try "pastéis de feijão," which are bean-based tarts. Still sweet, still delicious.

Amêijoas à Bulhão Pato

Amêijoas à Bulhão Pato is the dish you never knew you needed, but won't stop talking about once you've had it. We're talking clams, people. Clams sautéed in garlic, olive oil, and fresh cilantro, usually with a splash of white wine. It's named after a Portuguese poet, but the only poetry here is the dish itself.

Good to Know:

It's a popular appetizer, but let's be real, you'll want to order enough to make it a main dish. It's usually served with lemon wedges and sometimes bread to soak up the mouth-watering sauce.

Best Places to Eat:

"Ramiro" is iconic, but you'll also find locals loving this dish at "Cervejaria Trindade" or the laid-back "Ponto Final."

When to Eat:

Ideal for lunch or as a dinner starter, though you'll probably find yourself craving it at all hours.

Alternatives:

If clams aren't your thing, look for "mexilhões na cataplana" (mussels cooked in a copper pan with similar flavors).

Honestly, if you leave Lisbon without trying Amêijoas à Bulhão Pato, it's like leaving a music festival before the headliner comes on. Don't do it.

Alheira

Alheira is a Portuguese sausage that stands out for its unique mix of meats, which often doesn't include pork. This dish was a lifesaver for Portuguese Jews during the Inquisition, as it allowed them to eat "sausages" without breaking their dietary laws.

Good to Know:

It's typically smoked and then grilled or fried. The outer skin gets crispy, while the inside remains juicy and flavorful. It's often served with fried eggs and fries or rice, but some places get creative.

Best Places to Eat:

You can't go wrong with Alheira at "Tasca da Esquina" or "A Merendeira," spots where even the locals nod in approval.

When to Eat:

This is more of a dinner dish, though nobody's stopping you from enjoying it at lunch.

Alternatives:

If sausages have you yawning, try "Iscas com Elas," which is liver slices marinated in a white wine and garlic sauce, served with boiled potatoes.

To sum it up, Alheira is the culinary equivalent of that indie band everyone will claim to have "known about before they were popular." Don't miss out.

Frango Piri-Piri

Frango Piri-Piri is the Portuguese answer to the world's obsession with spicy chicken. Think of it as a barbecued chicken that went on a vacation to spice heaven and came back a changed bird.

Good to Know:

The term "Piri-Piri" actually refers to the pepper that gives this dish its kick. The chicken is marinated in a Piri-Piri sauce and then grilled to perfection.

Where to Eat:

Bonjardim, often called the Rei dos Frangos (King of Chickens), is a local favorite. If you want to escape touristy vibes, try Churrasqueira da Paz.

When to Eat:

Suitable for both lunch and dinner, but if you can handle the heat, why not both?

Alternatives:

If you're not into spicy food, many places offer a less fiery version, often called "Frango no Churrasco," which is grilled without the Piri-Piri marinade.

Lisbon's Vibrant Café Culture

Alright, let's be real: If you've been to Lisbon and haven't soaked up its café culture, did you even visit? Lisbon's café scene isn't just about sipping espresso; it's a mini-universe of social rituals, traditions, and, of course, tantalizing aromas.

The Classic Cafés:

These are your time capsules. Think Café A Brasileira with its Fernando Pessoa statue outside, or Martinho da Arcada, the oldest café in Lisbon where Portuguese poet Fernando Pessoa himself used to scribble verses. These spots serve more than coffee—they serve history in porcelain cups.

Kiosks & Quiosques:

Yeah, you read that right. These aren't your typical newsstands. Sprinkled throughout Lisbon's gardens and key intersections, these quiosques serve as impromptu social hubs. You'll find locals here sipping on 'galão' (a milky coffee) and 'bica' (espresso), discussing everything from football to fado music.

Coffee Lingo:

Walking into a Lisbon café without knowing the local coffee lingo is like going to a Metallica concert and asking them to play Taylor Swift. Get this straight: 'Bica' is your espresso, 'Meia-de-leite' is half milk, half coffee, and 'Abatanado' is your Americano.

Snacking Scene:

Coffee in Lisbon isn't a solo act; it comes with an ensemble of snacks. You're doing it wrong if you don't accompany your coffee with something savory or sweet. 'Tosta mista' (ham and cheese toastie) or the iconic Pastéis de Nata are popular choices.

Indie Cafés:

For those who enjoy being off the mainstream radar, Lisbon has seen a surge in indie coffee shops. They're serving specialty coffees, organic teas, and even vegan pastries. The Mill and Copenhagen Coffee Lab are among the spots redefining what Lisbon's café culture can offer.

Coffee and Culture:

Cafés in Lisbon are not just caffeine pit stops; they're mini cultural centers. You'll find cork boards with flyers of local events, live music nights, and even poetry readings. Some cafes like Ler Devagar in LX Factory double as bookstores!

Coffee in a Ginginha Cup?

Yes, you heard it right. In Lisbon, some daredevil souls take their espresso in an edible chocolate cup right after downing a 'Ginginha,' a local sour cherry liqueur. It's like a caffeinated roller coaster for your taste buds.

Lisbon's café culture is as complex as it is comforting. It's where the heart of the city beats, one coffee cup at a time. So, as you sip that aromatic brew, remember: you're part of a much larger, age-old Lisbon tradition. Cheers to that!

Key Takeaways

- Bacalhau à Brás is a must-try dish that's a unique take on codfish; check out restaurants in the Bairro Alto district.
- Pastéis de Nata is not just a snack but a cultural experience; find the freshest ones at Pastéis de Belém.
- Amêijoas à Bulhão Pato is for seafood lovers and pairs well with a glass of Vinho Verde.
- Alheira sausages are a tasty divergence from typical Portuguese cuisine, and no, it's not a Harry Potter spell.
- Frango Piri-Piri is your go-to comfort food; try it at a churrasqueira for an authentic experience.
- Lisbon's café culture is more than just about coffee; it's a social ritual that even includes unique language and pairing snacks.

Action Steps

- Eat Like a Local: Go to a "taverna" to experience an authentic meal.
- Time It Right: For Bacalhau à Brás, visit in the evening when the dish is freshest.
- Join the Queue: If there's a line outside a bakery selling Pastéis de Nata, join it, it's worth the wait.
- Tip for Quiosques: Carry small change for a quick coffee and snack at a local quiosque.
- Café Lingo: Learn a few local terms like "Bica" or "Meia-de-leite" to order coffee like a native.
- Discover Indie Cafés: Step into at least one specialty or indie café to experience the modern take on Lisbon's café culture.

Now that you've savored every culinary masterpiece Lisbon has to offer, it's time to digest it all to the beat of the city's vibrant nightlife. Trust me, you haven't lived until you've experienced Lisbon after dark. Turn the page, and let's dive into the night!

Chapter 4: Embracing Lisbon's Nightlife

"If there is one portion of Europe which was made by the sea more than another, Portugal is that slice, that portion, that belt. Portugal was made by the Atlantic."

– Hilaire Belloc

Lisbon doesn't go to sleep when the sun sets. No, no, my friend, the city just puts on its dancing shoes! From rooftop bars with views that'll make your heart soar, to underground clubs where the beats drop harder than my Wi-Fi connection, the night is where Lisbon truly comes alive. Buckle up, because we're about to embrace Lisbon's nightlife, and it's gonna be a wild ride!

Portugal's Traditional Music – Fado

If you haven't heard Fado music yet, let me be the first to say, you're in for an emotional journey that's as profound as any Scorsese film. Fado is not just music; it's the raw expression of the Portuguese soul. It's nostalgia, it's melancholy, it's longing, and joy—all packed into one soul-stirring experience.

Why You Must Listen to Fado

Ever had one of those nights where you just wanna sit down, sip on some wine, and let the world fade away? Fado is perfect for that. It's hauntingly beautiful, steeped in history, and culturally rich. Imagine the atmosphere—a dimly lit, intimate bar, the strumming of the Portuguese guitar, and a vocalist pouring their soul into every note.

Best Time to Experience Fado

Weekends are popular, but I'd recommend a weekday evening for a more intimate vibe. Most shows start around 9 or 10 PM, and there's often no cover charge—just pay for your drinks and perhaps a small tapas plate.

Insider Tips

- **Quiet Please:** During a Fado performance, talking is a no-no. This is soulful stuff, people! Let's give it the respect it deserves.
- **Café Luso or Clube de Fado?:** Both are legendary Fado houses. Café Luso is more touristy but a great introduction. Clube de Fado is for those who want to dig deeper.
- **No Need for Translation:** Seriously, even if you don't understand Portuguese, the emotion transcends language barriers.

Combo Deals

Hey, why not make a night of it? Many Fado venues are near the city's most iconic attractions. You can pair your cultural immersion with a bit of sightseeing before the night kicks off.

So, the next time someone asks you about your trip to Lisbon, and you start with, "Well, I listened to Fado music," you'll notice how the room goes quiet and how you've suddenly become the most interesting person in it. Trust me, it's an experience not to be missed.

Best Fado Houses: Where Tradition Lives

Alfama Fado House
- Why Go: For authentic Fado without the tourist hype.
- Location: Deep in the heart of Alfama.
- Insider Tip: Ask for a seat near the stage; they reserve the best spots for locals. Sneak your way into the in-crowd!

A Baiuca
- Why Go: For a community feel; even audience members sometimes get up to sing.
- Location: Also in Alfama, Lisbon's Fado epicenter.
- Insider Tip: It's cash-only, and they don't really have a menu. Just go with the flow.

Tasca do Chico
- Why Go: Popular among locals and tourists; Fado performances alternate with instrumental pieces.
- Location: Bairro Alto.
- Insider Tip: Arrive early or reserve a table because this place gets packed.

Contemporary Bars: Where Lisbon Lets Its Hair Down
- Pensão Amor
- Why Go: Think bohemian cabaret meets burlesque.
- Location: Cais do Sodré.
- Insider Tip: They have an amazing cocktail menu; try the 'Rosinha' for something uniquely Portuguese.

Park

- Why Go: A rooftop bar that gives new meaning to "urban jungle."
- Location: Calçada do Combro.
- Insider Tip: Go around sunset. You'll thank me later.

Cinco Lounge

- Why Go: For the cocktail aficionados.
- Location: Príncipe Real.
- Insider Tip: Let the bartender surprise you. Just tell them what flavors you like and watch them work their magic.

Bonus: Combo Places

Clube de Fado

- Why Go: Fado and fine dining in one. Great for a one-stop cultural evening.
- Location: Alfama (Yes, again! Alfama is where it's at for Fado).
- Insider Tip: Book a table in advance and ask for one near the stage. Don't say I didn't warn you—it's an emotional rollercoaster.

Povo

- Why Go: Offers Fado performances earlier in the evening, followed by DJ sets.
- Location: Cais do Sodré.
- Insider Tip: If you're looking to transition smoothly from soulful to soul-shaking, this is your spot. The vibe changes as the night progresses, so stick around.

Now, with Clube de Fado and Povo, you have two options where you can savor both traditional Fado and modern nightlife without hopping all over Lisbon. Both are magical in their own ways. Enjoy!

Tips for a Safe and Exciting Night Out in Lisbon

- **Stay Hydrated:** Seriously, a sip of water between drinks saves lives and mornings.
- **Cash & Card:** Always have some cash, but don't carry all your money with you. Many places accept cards, but having some euros on hand is smart.
- **The Buddy System:** It's an age-old tactic but effective. Keep an eye out for each other.
- **Local SIM or Roaming:** Ensure your phone is fully charged and you have a way to make calls or access GPS.
- **Know Basic Portuguese Phrases:** Like "ajuda" (help) or "onde é" (where is).
- **Avoid Dimly Lit Areas:** Stick to well-lit streets and bustling areas.
- **Keep an Eye on Your Drink:** You know why.
- **Public Transport Vs. Taxi/Ubers:** After midnight, public transport options are limited. Keep a taxi app or the number for a reliable taxi service handy.
- **Mind the Cobblestones:** Lisbon's streets can be uneven. Wear comfortable shoes that you can also dance in.
- **Legal Stuff:** Know the local laws, especially those related to drinking and public behavior.

Key Takeaways

- Fado music is an integral part of Lisbon's soul.
- Lisbon's café culture is more than just coffee; it's an experience.
- Lisbon offers a diverse culinary scene, from traditional dishes to modern cuisine.
- Nightlife in Lisbon can be both safe and thrilling if you follow the right precautions.

Action Steps

- Book a table in advance at a reputable Fado house to ensure you get the full experience.
- Find local cafes where you can enjoy an authentic Pastéis de Nata and café experience.
- Sample a variety of Portuguese dishes, from Bacalhau à Brás to Alheira.
- Follow safety guidelines while enjoying Lisbon's nightlife, like keeping an eye on your belongings and staying in well-lit areas.

Conclusion

So, we've hit the winding road together, folks—tasting, hearing, and literally walking through the ins and outs of Lisbon. If you've been riding along from the first page, I bet you're now a self-proclaimed bacalhau connoisseur, a Fado lyricist at heart, and a tram navigator worthy of a Lisbonite salute. But before you pack your bags and say adeus to this sun-kissed city, let's hit the pause button and look at a few final bits of wisdom. Think of this as the post-credits scene of your favorite show, except without a cliffhanger.

You've had your Lisbon adventure—from Pastéis de Nata sugar highs to the echoes of Fado in the narrow Alfama alleys. You've seen how this city weaves modern thrills with historic threads and serves it on a plate of delicious cuisine. But like any decent food platter, it leaves you craving a bit more. That's the thing about Lisbon; no matter how much you explore, there's always another cobblestone path whispering your name, another scenic overlook calling for a selfie.

Tips for the Next Leg of Your Journey

Let's say you're bitten by the travel bug and Lisbon was just the appetizer (a very hearty one at that). You'll want to savor more, right? First off, keep those comfy shoes. Portuguese hills aren't going anywhere, and neither are you without good footwear. Second, keep that digital phrasebook handy. 'Obrigado' and 'por favor' will get you far but learning a few more phrases might win you a free drink or a life story from a local, you never know.

If you've gotten a hang of navigating trams and hilly terrain, you're more than ready for any place. Got room in your suitcase? Pack a cork product, a can of sardines, or maybe even a Fado CD for that nostalgic ride back home. And while you're at it, jot down some places you missed because let's be honest, a second round in Lisbon wouldn't be a bad idea, would it?

Porto is Up Next!

Ready to turn the page? Literally. Because, after Lisbon, we're taking a scenic train ride up to Porto. Imagine the misty Douro River, barrels of port wine, and a certain blue-and-white tiled charm that only Porto can offer. But that's another story, and if you think Lisbon was an adventure, just wait till we get knee-deep into Porto's Ribeira District.

To wrap up this joyride through Lisbon, I'll leave you with this: adventure is a dish best served spontaneously, but a sprinkle of planning never hurt anyone. Until we meet again, whether it's on a Lisbon hilltop at sunset or navigating Porto's riverbanks, keep that wanderlust brewing and those taste buds tingling.

Ready for Porto? Hang tight, because we're just getting started!

BOOK 2

Porto Travel Guide

Explore to Win

Introduction

Are you on the hunt for that perfect honeymoon spot or just a slice of romance to spice up your life? Look no further, because Porto is where love stories get their happy endings, or rather, their enchanting beginnings. Nestled along the Douro River, Porto is known as Portugal's capital of charm, and it's not shy about it.

In Porto, every alleyway and river bend is ready for its close-up, begging to be in your next profile pic. It's a colorful storybook city, where the buildings are decked out in azulejos—those blue and white tiles that tell tales without saying a word.

Let's zoom in on the Ribeira. Imagine houses painted every shade under the sun, with clothes drying on balconies like flags of everyday life. It's where the city's pulse beats loudest, echoing off the Douro River. And when the sun sets, it's like the city's dipped in gold.

Now, Porto's not just a pretty face. This city knows its way around a kitchen—and a cellar. The smell of fresh-baked pastries mixes with the deep notes of port wine. You've got to try a francesinha if you're hungry: it's like a sandwich that dreams of becoming a feast.

And the wine—oh, the wine! Porto's the home of port wine, and it's everywhere. Take a sip, and you're tasting history and tradition.

Porto is also a bridge between the past and present. The Dom Luís I Bridge is a towering iron masterpiece, a walkway, and a monument all in one. It's got the best view in town—perfect for that epic selfie or just to gaze out and daydream.

But hey, what's a city without its nightlife? Porto's nights are alive with music and laughter. From cozy bars where the wine flows freely to clubs where you can dance till dawn, there's a beat for every mood. And the people? They'll welcome you like family, share their tales, and make sure your glass is never empty.

As the night winds down, you'll find Porto's still got you wrapped around its finger. It's a city that feels like a warm hug, a place that holds you close and whispers, "Stay a little longer."

So come on over. Walk down its alleys, breathe in the sea air, and let Porto work its magic. You'll eat, you'll drink, you'll dance, and you'll leave with memories wrapped in a ribbon of nostalgia.

In the pages to come, we'll explore every nook, taste every flavor, and get to the heart of what makes Porto, well, Porto. It's more than just a stop on your itinerary; it's a chapter in your travel story you'll want to read over and over.

But let's talk about you for a second. You might be thinking, "Another city, another list of sights to check off." Maybe you're worried about getting lost in yet another tourist trap, spending your precious time on experiences that don't feel authentic. Or perhaps you're concerned about missing out on the hidden spots that really tell the story of a place. We've all been there, staring at a monument and thinking, "Is this it?"

Fear not, intrepid traveler. This guide is your antidote to the common travel woes. We'll steer clear of the trampled paths and dive straight into the heart and soul of Porto. The goal? To give you an experience that's as rich and layered as the city itself. We're talking about the spots that locals love, the food that they eat, and the music they sway to. This isn't about scratching the surface; it's about diving in deep.

So, as we turn the page to this next chapter of your journey, keep this in mind: Porto is not just a place to visit. It's a place to feel. To laugh. To live. And this guide? It's your roadmap to all the feels and wonders Porto has to offer. Ready to fall in love with a city all over again? Porto is patiently waiting, and trust me, it's going to be unforgettable.

Chapter 1: Porto - The City by the Douro

"Porto is a living, breathing artwork."

– Siza Vieira

Craving a city that wraps you in its arms and tells you stories by the river? Welcome to Porto, the city that rises from the riverbanks of the Douro like a pop-up book fantasy.

Here, the old-world shakes hands with the new. At first glance, it's all about the grandeur of ancient churches and the timeless rhythm of laundry swaying in the breeze. But give it a minute, and you'll catch the undercurrent of youthful energy that courses through its narrow streets. So, buckle up—Porto's ready to take you on a ride you won't forget.

Porto's history isn't just written in books; it's poured into glasses worldwide. This city didn't just give its name to Port wine; it launched a flavor revolution that crossed oceans.

Port Wine: A Global Phenomenon

Origin: Back in the 17th century, Porto said, "Let's make wine," and the world never looked back.

The Big Change: When traders added a splash of brandy to stabilize wine for the journey to England, little did they know they were creating a global star.

Impact: Today, ask for Port wine anywhere from New York to New Delhi, and you'll get a taste of Porto's legacy.

Did You Know?

- Porto's wine cellars aren't just storages; they're treasure troves of history and oak-scented secrets.
- The Douro Valley, where the grapes are grown, is one of the oldest wine regions in the world.

- Port wine comes in several styles: Ruby, Tawny, White, and Rosé. That's right, Rosé!
- There's a Port wine for every palate, from sweet and red to complex and aged.

Porto's Timeline with Port Wine

- **1600s:** Trade wars with France open the doors for Portuguese wine in England.
- **1700s:** The Marquis of Pombal sets up the first appellation system in the world to regulate Port wine quality.
- **1800s:** Port wine becomes a British after-dinner favorite.
- **1900s:** Port wine evolves with modern times, but the traditional methods still reign supreme.

Next time you're swirling that glass of rich, red Port, remember: you're not just sipping on wine; you're sipping on history. Cheers to that!

Porto's past is as rich and varied as the port wine it's famous for. Here's a snapshot:

Porto's Historical Tapestry:

- Porto has been a bustling trade hub since Roman times—talk about old-school cool.

- The Moors left their mark too before being shown the door by King Ferdinand I.
- In the 14th century, Porto's shipbuilders were the unsung heroes behind the Age of Discovery.
- Fast forward to the 19th century, and Porto's industrial prowess had it nicknamed 'The Manchester of Portugal.'

The Architectural Mixtape:

- Check out the Clérigos Tower, an 18th-century marvel that's like the city's own baroque rocket ship to the clouds.
- São Bento Station isn't just a train station; it's a gallery of azulejo tiles telling Porto's history.
- The Dom Luís I Bridge is a double-decker iron wonder that had Gustave Eiffel's apprentice's fingerprints all over it.

Lesser-Known Facts About Porto's Architecture:

- Ever heard of the 'Armazéns?' These historic warehouses have morphed into cool shops and lofts.
- The Bolhão Market isn't just a place to buy fish; it's an Art Nouveau hotspot for foodies and photographers.
- Even Porto's McDonald's is a stunner—it's housed in the historic Café Imperial building with its Art Deco vibes.

The Nooks and Crannies:

- The Virtudes Garden is a stairway of green with city views that'll make your Instagram followers green with envy.
- Lello Bookstore is a gothic gem that would make any wizard feel at home, with a staircase that's a real-life optical illusion.

Porto's Architectural Journey:

- Medieval Times: Narrow alleys and sturdy walls—it was all about defense.
- Baroque Boom: The 18th century saw Porto get its grand makeover, adding flair to its religious buildings.
- Industrial Age: Come the 19th century, Porto was flexing with bridges and modern buildings that showcased its industrial clout.

Porto isn't just a feast for the eyes; it's a city with manners to match and celebrations for every calendar corner.

Local Etiquettes:

- **The Greeting:** A simple 'Bom dia' (Good morning) or 'Boa tarde' (Good afternoon) opens more doors than you think.
- **At the Table:** Don't rush your meal. Porto's dining is slow and savory—savor it.
- **On the Street:** Keep to the right on sidewalks and let the hurried locals pass.
- **In Conversation:** Porto folk are friendly but appreciate a bit of personal space. Handshakes are common, hugs not so much, unless you've hit it off.

Festivals to Jump Into:

- **São João Festival:** Picture this—every June, the city erupts in a carnival of hammers (yes, soft, plastic hammers), garlic flowers, and fireworks. It's like Mardi Gras with a Portuguese twist.
- **Porto Book Fair:** Bookworms unite every September in the gardens of Palácio de Cristal. It's a literary feast with a side of stunning views.

- **Festa de São Bartolomeu:** August brings the beach to life with an age-old tradition—bathing in the sea for good luck. It's chilly but charming.

Lesser-Known Celebrations:

- **Queima das Fitas:** In May, students celebrate the end of the academic year with parades and regalia. Think of it as a graduation party, city-wide.
- **Regata de Barcos Rabelos:** This June boat race on the Douro is not your average regatta. These are traditional port wine boats, and they're racing for glory.

Porto's etiquettes and festivals are as much a part of the city as its cobblestones and tiles. They're the heartbeat, the rhythm, the moves in the dance of daily life here. So, join in the festivities, raise your glass (or hammer) to the sky, and let Porto show you how to party. And remember, there's still more Porto to peel back. Stay tuned.

Key Takeaways

- **Porto's History:** A bustling trade hub since Roman times, it's a city that's played a pivotal role in global explorations and trade, especially known for its sweet, fortified port wine.

- **Architectural Heritage:** From the towering Clérigos Church to the azulejo-tiled beauty of São Bento Station and the industrial strength of the Dom Luís I Bridge, Porto's architecture tells the story of its past.

- **Hidden Architectural Gems:** Don't miss the Armazéns, the Bolhão Market, and even the ornate McDonald's at the historic Café Imperial for unique Art Nouveau and Art Deco experiences.

- **Cultural Etiquette:** Embrace the local customs, from greetings to dining. Engage with the city and its people respectfully and with patience.

- **Festivals:** Dive into the local culture by participating in Porto's festivals. Whether it's the boisterous São João Festival or the literary feast at the Porto Book Fair, there's a celebration for everyone.

- **Local Celebrations:** Get to know Porto's heart through less-known festivities like Queima das Fitas and the Regata de Barcos Rabelos, where tradition and community spirit shine.

Action Steps

- **Join the Table:** If you're invited for a meal, accept graciously. Take your time with the food, savor every bite, and join in the conversation.

- **Stroll With Awareness:** On Porto's streets, blend in with the locals. Keep to the right, be mindful of the pace, and always pass with politeness.

- **São João Festival:** Plan your trip around June to experience this unique festival. Buy a plastic hammer and join in the fun— it's a Porto rite of passage.

- **Book Fair and Literary Events:** If you're a literary enthusiast like me, schedule your visit for September to immerse yourself in the Porto Book Fair.

- **Watch the Boat Race:** If you're in Porto in June, catch the Regata de Barcos Rabelos to see traditional port wine boats in action.

That's a wrap on the first act of our Porto escapade, where history meets modernity and every corner has a story. But don't put your explorer's hat away just yet. There's more to this city than meets the eye, and we're just getting started.

Coming up, we'll step through the ornate doors of Livraria Lello, scale the heights of Clérigos Tower, and meander through the Ribeira District's lively lanes. We've got art, we've got music, and we've got festivals that transform the city into a stage.

Stick with me, and we'll unearth the hidden spots that make Porto the gem that it is. Ready for more? Let's turn the page and dive into the sights and sounds of Porto's soul.

Chapter 2: Porto's Landmarks, Festivals, and Hidden Wonders

"Any Portuguese town looks like bride's finery – something old, something new, something borrowed, and something blue."

– Mary Mccarthy

Chapter 2 is your VIP pass to Porto's heart and soul. We're peeling back the cobblestones to reveal the true character of this city. From the spellbinding shelves of Livraria Lello to the sky-high Clérigos Tower, get ready for an up-close-and-personal encounter with Porto's most iconic landmarks.

But it doesn't stop at postcard sights. Porto's pulse is felt strongest in its vibrant festivals and secret spots, hidden from the typical tourist trail. Ready for an authentic slice of Porto life? Let's dive in and experience the city's legendary joie de vivre together.

Livraria Lello

Livraria Lello is a bookworm's dream with a twist. This century-old bookstore is famous for its neo-gothic façade and a stunning red staircase that sweeps you up in a literary embrace. It's rumored to have inspired J.K. Rowling's descriptions of Hogwarts, making it a pilgrimage site for Potterheads worldwide.

Step inside, and it's a feast for the eyes: stained-glass windows light up the carved wood, and books reach up to the ornate ceiling. It's not just about what's on the shelves; the store itself is a masterpiece.

Why Visit: It's a living museum where literature takes the main stage. And that staircase—it's a star in its own right.

Getting There: Nestled in the heart of downtown Porto, it's a short walk from the São Bento train station.

What to Do: Browse the shelves, soak in the ambiance, and climb the famous stairs for a top-down view of the store.

Not to Miss: The stained-glass skylight. It's a piece of art that bathes the bookstore in a complex pattern of colors.

Insider Tips:

- Buy a book as your ticket to enter—it's a souvenir and your pass rolled into one.
- Go early or during off-peak hours to avoid the crowds.
- Use the side door if you just want to visit the café and avoid the entrance queue.

Clérigos Tower

Clérigos Tower reaches skyward, a baroque tower with a view that captures Porto's charm in one sweeping glance. Climbing the 240 steps rewards you with a breeze that carries tales of the city and a vista that stretches to the horizon.

The Fame: Known for being one of Porto's tallest landmarks, the tower offers a bird's-eye perspective on the city's intricate layout.

The Look: Ascend the granite staircase that winds tightly to the summit, where the cityscape awaits your awe.

Why Worth a Visit: The climb pays off with a panoramic spectacle of Porto's undulating landscape, river, and beyond.

Getting There: Nestled in the Vitória neighborhood, it's an easy stroll from central landmarks and transport hubs.

What to Do: Conquer the tower, capture the view, and check out the church's acoustics, perhaps during one of its intimate concerts.

Don't Miss: The chance to watch the city light soften into twilight hues from the peak.

Insider Tips:

- Opt for a combo ticket with the church and museum for a more comprehensive experience.
- Clear days are your friend here for the most Instagram-worthy snaps.
- Comfort is key—choose footwear wisely for the ascent.

Clérigos Tower offers more than a lofty perch; it's a stairway to a richer connection with Porto.

The Ribeira District

Ribeira is the kind of place where postcards are jealous of real life. Down by the Douro, life's a parade of open-air cafes, street artists sketching the day away, and boats bobbing like apples in a tub.

Meet the Neighbors: Colorful homes line up like old friends sharing tales of the sea. They stand tall with years of stories carved into their walls.

Why You Must Visit: Riberia is where you come to see the real Porto in motion – fishermen hauling in their catch, grandmas haggling over fresh produce, and kids using ancient steps as their personal playgrounds.

Best Time to Visit: Dusk. That's when Ribeira dresses up in golden hour finery, and the cafes spill over with chatter, clinking glasses, and the scent of roasted octopus.

Handy Information

- **Location:** Hugging the Douro, it's the heartbeat of downtown Porto.
- **Time to Spend:** Give it a few hours or, better yet, a full evening.
- **Public Transport:** The D-line of the metro drops you off at São Bento, and it's just a hop, skip, and jump away.
- **Facilities:** Ribeira's got everything from traditional taverns to hipster bars and artisan shops.

Insider Tips

- **Grab a Bite:** The local tascas serve up Porto on a plate – cheap, cheerful, and oh-so-tasty.
- **Music to Your Ears:** You'll often find impromptu live music. Follow the melody; it's usually a free show.
- **Take a Cruise:** Hop on one of the rabelo boats for a river-eye view of the district.
- **Safety:** It's bustling and bright, but keep your wits about you as the night wears on.

Budget Tips

- **Sip Smart:** The backstreet bars serve up Super Bock and Vinho Verde without the riverside markup.
- **Eat Local:** Sidestep the tourist menus and munch on petiscos (Portuguese tapas) for a flavorful bargain.

So, Ribeira's ready for you – with open arms and a full glass. Are you ready to join the party?

São Bento Railway Station

Next on our tour of Porto's heartbeats is the São Bento Railway Station. Don't mistake it for a mere pit stop or a transient space. São Bento tells a story, right there on its walls, with over 20,000 azulejo tiles that illustrate Portugal's history. It's a gallery of blue and white, where scenes of battles, royalty, and the daily grind of past centuries freeze in glossy ceramic.

Why It's a Must-See:
- It's a cultural hub. Those tiles? They're the silent narrators of Portugal's past.
- The architecture is a spectacle—a blend of French Beaux-Arts and Portuguese flair.

The Visual Feast: Look out for the main frieze above the train schedule. It's a timeline of transport, from horse-drawn carriages to steam trains.

Visiting Details:
- **Where:** Right in the center of Porto, hard to miss.
- **Best Time:** Mornings are great for photos without the rush.

Travel Tip: It's a working station, so keep an eye on the time if you're catching a train!

What to Do There:
- Take in the grand entrance hall, and let those tiles transport you through time.
- Find the historical depictions of the Battle of Valdevez and King João I.

Never Miss: The detail. Each tile, each scene, has a nuance waiting to be discovered.

Insider Insights:
- Pop by the station café for a coffee with a view of the tiles—it's like a live history book with your espresso.
- Just outside, the Porto Tram picks up, offering a nostalgic ride through the city.

São Bento Railway Station is where journeys begin and stories unfold, all under one ornate roof. It's a cornerstone of Porto's identity and a must-visit for any traveler looking to connect with the city's soul.

Art of Porto

Porto's art scene is as vibrant and varied as the city itself. Let's take a closer look at the galleries and spaces that paint the most accurate picture of Porto's artistic heartbeat.

Espaco Mira: Tucked away in the artistic neighborhood of Campanhã, Espaco Mira is a beacon for contemporary art lovers. This gallery is where the new and adventurous come to light. With its rotating exhibitions, it's never the same place twice.

- **What to Love:** It's a space that challenges your perspectives, often showcasing multimedia installations.
- **Insider Tip:** Check out Mira Forum, its sister gallery across the street, for photography exhibitions.

Serralves Museum: This isn't just a museum; it's a statement piece of modern art itself, nestled in a lush park. The Serralves is where you go to see world-class exhibitions and works by both Portuguese and international artists.

- **What to Love:** The art deco villa and the contemporary main building make it a dual delight of history and modernity.

- **Insider Tip:** Don't miss the museum's park—it's a living, green gallery with sculptures that will make your walk an artistic discovery.

Galeria Fernando Santos: This is one of the most respected galleries in Porto, bridging the gap between emerging talents and established names. It's a place of dialogue between the artist and the public.

- **What to Love:** It's known for nurturing local artists and has played a pivotal role in Porto's art scene since the '90s.
- **Insider Tip:** Attend an opening if you can; it's a who's who of Porto's art world.

Galeria Nuno Centeno: Once known as Reflexus Arte Contemporânea, this gallery has rebranded and reshaped itself into a hub for cutting-edge art. Here, innovation and expression collide in a celebration of contemporary movements.

- **What to Love:** It's edgy and unapologetic, often showcasing avant-garde pieces.
- **Insider Tip:** Keep an eye on their calendar for curator talks and unique performance art shows.

Porto's art scene is a canvas of creativity, and these spaces are just the beginning. Each offers a unique glimpse into the artistic soul of the city, telling Porto's story through strokes of genius and splashes of color.

Music of Porto

In Porto, music leaps from the shadows of every alley, turning the whole city into a stage. It's a city that doesn't just sing; it invites you to join the chorus.

Casa da Música: Shaped like a geometric wonder, Casa da Música is the architectural wonder of concert halls. This venue is the core of Porto's music scene, offering everything from classical to cutting-edge electronic.

- **What to Love:** The acoustics here are world-class—every note feels like it's played just for you.
- **Insider Tip:** Take a guided tour of the building to uncover its design secrets before settling down for a performance.

Coliseu Porto: This grand old dame of a theater is where history meets high notes. It's seen the likes of everything from operas to rock concerts, and it's a visual and auditory feast.

- **What to Love:** The vintage charm here is profound; you'll feel like you've stepped back in time.
- **Insider Tip:** Check out their lineup for a night where you can dress up and dive into the past.

Hot Five Jazz & Blues Club: Tucked away in the heart of the city, this club is a haven for those who like their music with soul. The Hot Five is intimate, brimming with character, and always swinging with live jazz and blues.

- **What to Love:** It's the real deal for jazz aficionados— improvised, spontaneous, and utterly captivating.
- **Insider Tip:** Arrive early to grab a seat close to the stage; the place fills up fast when local favorites are playing.

Plano B: A hybrid space that's part gallery, part club, Plano B beats to the rhythm of Porto's contemporary pulse. By day it's an art space; by night, the lower level morphs into a vibrant club where DJs spin the latest tracks.

- **What to Love:** It's the epitome of Porto's modern side, where music and art collide in the coolest way.

- **Insider Tip:** Explore the whole venue—the upstairs area offers a more laid-back vibe with a great cocktail menu.

Porto's music venues are as diverse as the genres they celebrate. Each one offers a different flavor of the city's soundscape, from the classical music in the Casa da Música to the soulful strums in the Hot Five. So let your ears lead the way and discover the rhythms that make Porto truly dance.

Hidden Attractions of Porto

Miragaia

Why You Must Visit

Tucked behind the splashier Ribeira, Miragaia is where the paint's chipped just right, and every turn is a nod to Porto's past life. It's less about the postcard and more about the story. Here, the Douro is your soundtrack, and locals might just spill secrets over a glass of Vinho Verde.

Best Time to Visit

Catch it in the late afternoon when the sun plays tag with the shadows, and the river starts to sparkle.

Handy Information

- **Location:** Steps away from the river, stretching under the lofty gaze of the Arrábida Bridge.
- **Opening Hours:** It's an open neighborhood, so come whenever, but some spots keep a typical 9-5 hours.
- **Ticket Price:** Walking around is free; experiences may vary.
- **Time to Spend:** Set aside a couple of hours to meander properly.

- **Public Transport:** The tram will get you close, then your feet do the rest.
- **Parking:** A bit of a challenge, it's easier to walk or ride in.
- **Facilities:** Snug cafes and quirky shops make for perfect pit stops.

Insider Tips

- **Snack Stops:** Grab a 'francesinha' sandwich at a local joint and join the debate about who makes the best one.
- **Stroll Strategy:** Let the lanes guide you; Miragaia's layout is a treasure map you'll want to follow without a compass.
- **Riverfront Relaxing:** The promenade is perfect for a sunset gander.
- **Workshop Wandering:** The artisans here are friendly; pop in to see their crafts and stories unfold.

Virtudes Park (Jardim das Virtudes)

Why You Must Visit

This park is Porto's secret garden, a stacked series of terraces that locals treat like their backyard. It's a place where the grass whispers local tales, and the benches are seasoned with stories of old friends catching up.

Best Time to Visit

Late afternoon is golden. That's when the sun plays peek-a-boo with the leaves and the Douro twinkles like a sea of diamonds in the distance.

Handy Information

- **Location:** A hop away from the artsy Miguel Bombarda street.
- **Opening Hours:** It's always open, but it's at its best when the sun's out.

- **Ticket Price:** Free. The best things in life, right?
- **Time to Spend:** Give it an hour, or as long as you want to laze under the Porto sky.
- **Public Transport:** The area's well-connected, a short walk from Aliados Avenue will get you there.
- **Parking:** It's tight around Virtudes; your best bet is two feet and a heartbeat.
- **Facilities:** It's all about the views and vibes here, but cafes nearby will sort out your coffee fix.

Insider Tips

- **Picnic Spot:** Grab some take away from a nearby deli and find your spot on the grass.
- **Sunset Watch:** As the sky turns pink and orange, Virtudes Park is where you'll want to be.
- **Local Life:** It's not unusual to find an impromptu music session or a quiet artist sketching the scene.

Key Takeaways

- **Livraria Lello:** A must for book lovers and architecture enthusiasts, with its neo-gothic facade and iconic red staircase.

- **Clérigos Tower:** Offers the best panoramic views of Porto and a challenging but rewarding climb.

- **Ribeira District:** The heart of Porto's nightlife and a colorful display of the city's traditional architecture and riverside charm.

- **São Bento Railway Station:** Not just a transport hub but a historical monument adorned with azulejo tile artwork depicting Portugal's history.

- **Art Scene:** Porto's galleries, like Espaco Mira and Serralves Museum, are hotspots for contemporary art and cultural exhibitions.

- **Music Venues:** Casa da Música and Coliseu Porto are key for experiencing the city's diverse and dynamic music scene, from classical concerts to modern beats.

- **Hidden Gems:** Miragaia offers a less-touristy, authentic neighborhood experience, while Virtudes Park is the perfect sunset spot for a quiet retreat.

Action Steps

- **Book Ahead:** For Livraria Lello, reserve your ticket online to skip the long lines and ensure a spot.

- **Step Count:** Before tackling Clérigos Tower, stretch those legs—it's a climb that'll count for your daily workout.

- **Evening Stroll:** Wander the Ribeira District as dusk falls to catch the neighborhood's transformation from quaint to electrifying.

- **Tile Gazing:** At São Bento Railway Station, take a moment to really look at the azulejo tiles—each one tells a part of Portugal's story.

- **Gallery Hop:** Set aside an afternoon to explore Porto's art galleries; they often have free entry times or days.

- **Live Tunes:** Check Casa da Música's schedule for free concerts or rehearsals open to the public.

- **Off the Beaten Path:** In Miragaia, let curiosity guide you—this district rewards the wanderer with hidden cafes and stunning views.

- **Sunset Pause:** Time your visit to Virtudes Park just before sunset for an unforgettable end to your day.

And just like that, we danced across the cobblestones, and climbed the towers of Porto's most captivating corners. Next up, we're diving fork-first into the city's culinary soul. Get ready to savor the flavors that make Porto a true foodie's haven—from the spicy tang of a francesinha to the sweet, velvety texture of pastel de nata. Let's keep this adventure rolling and taste our way through the next delicious chapter!

Chapter 3: Porto's Culinary Scene

You know you're Portuguese when you called any pasta "shpargett"

-LPC

Chapter 3 is where Porto's true flavor comes to life. Here, every dish tells a story, every sip carries a tradition, and every bite is a celebration. Prepare your taste buds for a journey through a culinary landscape as rich and varied as the city's tiled façades. We're about to uncover the tastes that define Porto, from the smoky scent of grilled sardines by the Douro to the spicy whispers of piri-piri in tucked-away tavernas. Let's eat our way through Porto's delicious secrets, one mouth-watering morsel at a time.

Tradition of Port Wine

We have discussed the background of Port wine; now let's explore the finest ways to enjoy it.

- **Ruby Port:** Young, vibrant, and fruit-forward, Ruby Port loves the company of chocolate desserts or a cheese board featuring robust cheeses like aged cheddar or blue cheese. It's the life of the party on any dessert table.

- **Tawny Port:** More complex and mellow, Tawny is your go-to for creamy desserts, caramel-rich sweets, or even a plate of savory roasted nuts. Picture it alongside a crème brûlée, and you're in for a symphony of flavors.

- **White Port:** Crisp and versatile, White Port is a refreshing aperitif that pairs delightfully with olives, salted almonds, or a fresh seafood dish. Serve it chilled for a zesty start to any meal.

- **Rosé Port:** The newcomer in the port family, Rosé Port is a fun twist with its berry flavors making it a great match for fruit-based desserts or even a simple scoop of vanilla ice cream.

But where do you find the best wine? Porto is a treasure trove of wine experiences, and the best sips aren't always found in the most obvious places.

Wine Shops for the Connoisseur:

- **Garrafeira do Carmo:** This cozy shop is a favorite for those in the know. Walls lined with bottles, it's like a library for wine. Ask the owner for a recommendation; they love to share hidden gems.
- **Vinho & Coisas:** A boutique store with knowledgeable staff, perfect for finding that special bottle to take home or enjoy by the riverbank.

Local Markets for a Laid-back Taste:

- **Mercado do Bolhão:** Amidst the hustle, you'll find stalls selling local wines. It's a chance to chat with vendors and maybe snag a bottle or two at a friendly price.
- **Mercado de Matosinhos:** A bit further out, but here you can pair fresh market finds with a bottle chosen from local stalls.

Wine Bars for the Social Sipper:

- **Prova - Wine, Food & Pleasure:** A chic spot where the staff will guide you through a tasting flight tailored to your preferences.
- **Capela Incomum:** A wine bar in a converted chapel, offering a divine selection of wines and a unique atmosphere.

Wineries Just a Trip Away:

- **Taylor's Port Wine Cellars:** Across the river in Vila Nova de Gaia, Taylor's offers tours and tastings with stunning views.
- **Graham's Port Lodge:** Another Gaia highlight, Graham's combines history with a modern tasting room and a beautiful terrace.

For the Full Experience:

- **Douro Valley Day Trips:** Consider a day trip up the river to the Douro Valley. Many wine tour operators offer visits to several wineries, complete with tastings and often lunch with a view of the terraced vineyards.

Insider Tips:

- **Tasting Over Buying:** In wine shops, ask if they offer tastings. You might discover your new favorite Port before committing to a bottle.
- **Festivals Are Key:** Time your visit with wine festivals like the Festa de São João for tastings and fun.
- **Ask Locals:** Strike up a conversation at a café or bar. Portuenses are proud of their wine and will point you to the best spots.

In Porto, the best wine isn't just found; it's experienced. It's shared stories, laughter around a bar, and the clink of glasses as the city toasts to yet another beautiful sunset.

Francesinha

The Francesinha sandwich is more than simply a meal; it's a symbol of Porto's commitment to robust flavors. It's a tower of bread, wet-cured ham, linguiça, fresh sausages like chipolata, steak, or roast meat, and draped in a blanket of melted cheese. The final flourish? A warm, beer-infused tomato sauce that cascades over the whole assembly, often with a fried egg perched on top.

Where to Eat:

- **Café Santiago:** Arguably the most famous spot in Porto for a Francesinha, it sticks to the classic recipe and has perfected the art.
- **Bufete Fase:** It's a no-frills joint, but their Francesinha has a loyal following for its authenticity and generous sauce.

Tips:

- **Sauce Savvy:** Each establishment has its own secret sauce recipe. Some like it spicy, others a bit sweeter. Don't be afraid to ask about the sauce before you dive in.
- **Pairing Perfect:** A cold Super Bock beer is the traditional accompaniment, cutting through the richness of the dish.
- **Timing is Everything:** Francesinha is a heavy dish, best enjoyed for lunch or an early dinner, giving you time to walk it off.
- **Variations:** Some places offer a vegetarian version, swapping out meats for veg-friendly alternatives without losing the essence of the dish.
- **Sharing? Maybe Not:** It's a dish meant for one, but if you're not super hungry, consider splitting it. Just be aware that for many locals, sharing a Francesinha is almost a sacrilege!

In Porto, tackling a Francesinha is a rite of passage. It's hearty, it's messy, and it's utterly delicious—a true reflection of the city's spirit on a plate.

Tripas à Moda do Porto

Tripas à Moda do Porto, or Tripe Porto Style, weaves a tale of sacrifice and invention. This dish dates back to the Age of Discoveries, when Porto's inhabitants supposedly offered all their meat to Henry the Navigator's expeditions, leaving only tripe for themselves. They turned necessity into a delicacy, and thus, this stew was born.

What It Is:

A robust stew that combines tripe with white beans, carrots, rice, and various types of meat, typically sausage and sometimes veal. It's slow-cooked to develop deep flavors and a tender texture.

Where to Eat:

- **Cozinha do Martinho:** This place has been serving traditional Portuguese fare for decades. Their Tripas à Moda do Porto is a testament to their commitment to tradition.
- **Gaveto:** Renowned for its seafood, O Gaveto also offers a stellar version of the tripe stew, honoring the authentic recipe.

Tips:

- **Acquired Taste:** Tripe isn't for everyone, but this dish could turn you into a believer. It's all about the slow cooking that melds the flavors together.
- **Local Pairing:** Try it with a glass of Douro red wine; the robust flavors of the stew are perfectly complemented by the wine's body and tannins.
- **Seasonal Enjoyment:** While available year-round, it's particularly satisfying in the cooler months.
- **Savor Slowly:** This is a dish that's meant to be enjoyed leisurely, soaking up the sauce with a piece of crusty bread.
- **Open-minded Approach:** If you're wary of tripe, this might just be the perfect introduction—cooked till it's meltingly soft and richly flavored.

Bacalhau à Gomes de Sá

Bacalhau à Gomes de Sá is a nod to Porto's seafaring history, a dish that speaks of the ocean's bounty and the city's love for simplicity and flavor. It's a casserole where salted cod, the star of Portuguese cuisine, is lovingly combined with thinly sliced potatoes, onions, hard-boiled eggs, olives, and garnished with a sprinkle of parsley. It's said that

José Luís Gomes de Sá, the son of a rich 19th-century cod trader, created this recipe.

Where to Eat:

- **A Grade:** A family-run establishment that prides itself on home-cooked flavors and has mastered this dish to perfection.
- **Restaurante Ora Viva:** Known for its traditional dishes, Ora Viva serves a Bacalhau à Gomes de Sá that's consistently praised by locals and visitors alike.

Tips:

- **Pair Wisely:** A glass of crisp Vinho Verde complements the dish's flavors and cuts through the richness.
- **Portion Sizes:** It's a hearty dish, so ensure your appetite is ready, or consider sharing if you're sampling multiple courses.
- **Authentic Experience:** Seek out places that specialize in traditional Portuguese cuisine for the most authentic version of the dish.
- **Advance Notice:** Some restaurants require you to order this dish in advance due to its lengthy preparation time.
- **Enjoy Every Bite:** Take time to savor the interplay of flavors—the salty fish, the creamy potatoes, and the freshness of the parsley all come together to tell a tale of Porto's culinary artistry.

Broa de Avintes

Broa de Avintes is a dense cornbread that hails from Avintes, a town in the Vila Nova de Gaia municipality near Porto. This bread is a robust companion to many Portuguese meals, particularly those with a rich, saucy character. It's dark, sometimes sweet, and with a distinct texture that comes from a mix of corn and rye flour.

Where to Eat:

- **Padaria Ribeiro:** A staple bakery in Porto known for its traditional bread. Their Broa de Avintes is authentic, with a perfect crust and hearty crumb.
- **Mercado do Bolhão:** In the bustling market, various vendors offer freshly baked Broa de Avintes. It's an opportunity to sample it straight from the oven.

Tips:

- **Pairing:** Broa de Avintes is ideal with soups and stews, as it soaks up flavors like no other bread.
- **Texture Delight:** Expect a crumbly texture, a world away from soft sandwich loaves. This bread is about substance and taste.
- **Tasting Note:** If you're new to Broa de Avintes, try it first without accompaniments to appreciate its unique flavor.
- **Storage:** Due to its density, Broa de Avintes lasts longer than most bread, so you can enjoy it over several days.
- **Local Secret:** Toast a slice and enjoy it with a smear of fresh butter or a slice of cheese for a simple yet delicious snack.

Bolinhos de Bacalhau

These tempting morsels, known as Bolinhos de Bacalhau, are one of Porto's signature treats. They are salt cod fritters, combining the ocean's harvest with the earthy goodness of potatoes, a hint of parsley, and a zesty kick of onion. The mixture is shaped into small ovals and fried until golden—a crunchy exterior giving way to a flaky, flavorful interior.

Where to Eat:

- **Casa Portuguesa do Pastel de Bacalhau:** They specialize in these fritters, pairing them with a glass of white port for a truly Porto experience.

- **Mercado de Matosinhos:** This local market offers some of the freshest Bolinhos de Bacalhau, as it's near the fishing port where the cod comes in.

Tips:

- **Dipping Sauce:** While delicious on their own, try them with a garlicky aioli or a tomato-based sauce to add another dimension of flavor.
- **Perfect Pair:** Bolinhos de Bacalhau and a cold Super Bock beer are a match made in Porto.
- **Eat Them Hot:** For the best experience, have them fresh out of the fryer when they're most crispy.
- **Try at Home:** Many shops sell them ready to cook, so you can enjoy these treats back in your own kitchen.
- **Local Gatherings:** They're a staple at Porto's festive gatherings, so if you're in town for a festival, you're likely to come across these bite-sized delights.

The Coffee and Bakery Culture of Porto

Visiting Porto's cafes and bakeries is like stepping into a warm hug from an old friend who just happens to bake the best pastries and brews the richest coffee. Here, the baristas know your life story by your second visit, and the pastries are always fresh, flaky, and calling your name.

Coffee Breaks Are a Ritual: In Porto, coffee isn't just a morning jolt; it's an art and a pause in the day. Cafés are the neighborhood's living rooms, where news is exchanged over espresso that's strong enough to kickstart a moped.

Bakeries Are Time Machines: Walking into a Porto bakery is like time-traveling to when things were simpler and sweeter. The display windows are like edible exhibits, with rows of pastel de nata, eclairs, and bolinhos that could outshine any jeweler's case.

Local Favorites:

- **Majestic Café:** Sure, it's known to travelers, but it's an icon for a reason. The Belle Époque décor is a feast for the eyes, and their coffee is the perfect accompaniment to people-watching.
- **Confeitaria do Bolhão:** This is old-school Porto at its best. Grab a pão de ló (sponge cake) or a biscoito (biscuit), and you'll see why locals have been loyal for generations.

Pro Tips:

- **Pastries:** They're not just for breakfast. A mid-afternoon bola de Berlim (cream-filled doughnut) can turn a regular day into a celebration.
- **Coffee Lingo:** Learn to order like a local. A 'cimbalino' is a shot of espresso, and a 'meia de leite' is akin to a latte.

Key Takeaways

- **Francesinha:** A Porto icon, this sandwich is a culinary adventure in itself. Find the best at Café Santiago or Bufete Fase and enjoy it with a beer.

- **Tripas à Moda do Porto:** A hearty and traditional stew that connects you to the city's history. Cozinha do Martinho and O Gaveto are the go-to spots for this authentic dish.

- **Bacalhau à Gomes de Sá:** A comfort dish featuring salted cod that's a staple on Porto tables. A Grade and Restaurante Ora Viva serve up some of the most authentic versions.

- **Broa de Avintes**: This dense, dark cornbread is a must-try for its unique texture and flavor. Look for it at Padaria Ribeiro or local markets like Mercado do Bolhão.

- **Bolinhos de Bacalhau:** These beloved cod fritters are perfect for snacking, available at Casa Portuguesa do Pastel de Bacalhau and Mercado de Matosinhos.

- **Coffee Culture:** It's a vital part of Porto's social fabric, with iconic cafes like Majestic Café and Confeitaria do Bolhão offering a window into the city's soul.

- **Bakery Scene:** Pastries are a portal to Porto's sweet side, with treats like pastel de nata and bola de Berlim found in bakeries city-wide.

Action Steps

- **Enjoy the Francesinha:** Head to Café Santiago to face off with this local legend. Remember, it's typically a solo endeavor, but no judgment if you want to share.

- **Savor the Stew:** Make your way to Cozinha do Martinho for a bowl of Tripas à Moda do Porto. It's a cozy place that feels like grandma's kitchen.

- **Cod Quest:** Visit A Grade for Bacalhau à Gomes de Sá. It's a dish best enjoyed with a glass of white wine and a side of history.

- **Bread Adventure:** Find the Broa de Avintes at Padaria Ribeiro. Buy a loaf to share—or not. It pairs well with cheese or jam.

- **Fritter Fix:** For the freshest Bolinhos de Bacalhau, hit up the stalls at Mercado de Matosinhos. They're crispy on the outside, fluffy on the inside, and perfect on the go.

- **Coffee Culture Dip:** Take a seat at Majestic Café. Order a cimbalino and a pastel de nata, and soak in the Belle Époque ambiance.

- **Pastel Pilgrimage:** Confeitaria do Bolhão is your spot for a mid-afternoon sweet treat. Try the éclairs, or go for a bola de Berlim.

We've feasted our way through Porto's culinary landscape, from the daring flavors of the Francesinha to the rich tradition in each spoonful of Tripas à Moda do Porto. You've sipped coffee where the poets mused and bitten into pastries straight from the oven. But our journey doesn't end at the dinner table.

Next up, we're stepping into the daily dance of Porto life in Chapter 4, "Living Like a Portuense." Get ready to walk the walk and talk the talk, embracing thelocal life, from shopping at neighborhood markets to cheering at a football match. On to Chapter 4 we go!

Chapter 4: Living Like a Portuense

"I grew up in Portugal, and people there party 'til 7 or 8 in the morning there."

– Sara Sampaio

There's no shame in being a visitor, but isn't it a thrill to blend in? To catch the early gossip of the market, to debate over the best bifana, to clink glasses where the only language you need is laughter. Let's roll out of bed, pull back the curtains, and see Porto not through the lens of a camera, but through the eyes that call it home. Ready to savor every second like a true Portuense? Let's go.

Bonfim

Bonfim is like that eccentric cousin who's always got a story to tell. The first time I wandered into Bonfim, I felt like I'd accidentally crashed a cool local's secret hangout. With its narrow streets adorned with street art, this place is like an open-air gallery where the buildings are the canvases and the residents are the curators. The first time I veered off into Bonfim, I was hunting for a cup of coffee and ended up in a poetry slam. Yeah, it's that kind of place.

Why You Can't Skip Bonfim:

- **Art Overload:** At every corner, you're likely to bump into a mural or a makeshift gallery in someone's garage.
- **Café Culture:** The coffee spots here serve up more than your average espresso; expect baristas who double as local historians.

- **Vintage Finds:** Thrift shops where you can snag a 70s leather jacket or a vinyl that's been waiting just for you.
- **Community Feel:** Everyone seems to know everyone, and it won't be long before they're giving you tips on the best pastel de nata in town.

Where and What:

- **Rua do Bonfim:** The main drag where you can pop into a cozy café like Café Candelabro, a spot that's half bookstore, half caffeine heaven.
- **The Old Factory:** Now an art collective, where once they made bread, now they're cooking up cultural feasts with exhibitions and live music nights.
- **The Community Garden:** A patch of green where locals grow veggies and the occasional concert blooms under the stars.

Getting There: Bonfim is just a stone's throw from the iconic Ponte de Dom Luís I. Hop on the metro to Campo 24 de Agosto station, and you're practically there.

So, why wander into Bonfim? Because sometimes, you need a dose of real, raw, heart-on-its-sleeve Porto. And who knows, you might just leave with a new favorite poem in your pocket and the aftertaste of the best coffee you've had in ages.

Cedofeita

Cedofeita is the kind of neighborhood that winks at you from across the Douro. It's where tradition elbows the future and says, "Make room, I've got stories to tell." I swear the cobblestones here are part muse, part mischief—each one has a knack for tripping you into a new adventure.

The last time I sauntered down Rua Miguel Bombarda, which is Cedofeita's answer to a bohemian dream, I was on a mission for a rare vinyl. I ducked into a record shop, and voila! The jazz and indie pop music made the two hours fly by. Walk a little further, and you'll find a café where they serve up lattes with a side of live poetry, and the barista doubles as a philosopher.

Why Cedofeita Can't Be Missed:

- **Indie Galleries:** They don't just display art; they throw you into it. Think of Rosa Imunda, where the paint is still wet and the welcome is warm.
- **Caffeine Corners:** Like the snug Mimosa, where the coffee is strong and the pastries come with a backstory—usually involving a grandmother's secret recipe.
- **Boutique Bingo:** It's a treasure hunt here. My favorite leather bag? It's from a hole-in-the-wall that whispered my name as I wandered past.

Finding Your Way:

A hop and a skip from the city center, or a metro ride to Carolina Michaelis—follow the scent of fresh bread and the sound of the local band rehearsing.

Baixa

Baixa is Porto's smile – wide, welcoming, and full of stories. The busy center area is where you can hear a mix of business and culture with every step. And let me tell you, it's the kind of place where you can find me grabbing an espresso at Café Guarany on Avenida dos Aliados, a spot with a vibe as grand as the avenue itself.

Here's why Baixa should be scribbled in bold on your must-visit list:

The Market: If you go to the Mercado do Bolhão, you'll hear people laughing and bargaining over the freshest food this side of the Douro. And hey, ever had a bifana that makes you want to write a love letter? Grab one at Tascö and start drafting!

Shop, Sip, Stare: Take a jaunt down Rua de Santa Catarina. Shop? Sure. But also sip on some fine Douro wine at a street-side café and stare at the world going by. Need a breather? The art nouveau gem Café Majestic is your time machine to the roaring twenties.

When the Stars Come Out: Galerias Paris by night is where Baixa lets its hair down. Want the real Porto vibe? Duck into Plano B, a bar where the locals become your besties by the end of the night.

Culture with a Side of Drama: São João National Theatre is the grand dame of culture. Pop in for a show; it's worth it just for the gasps at the gilded interior.

Finding Baixa: Hop off at the Aliados metro station. You can't miss it – just follow the noise!

Recommendations For Shopping, Crafts, and Souvenirs

For shopping in Porto that's as authentic as it gets, you need to hit the local markets and traditional shops. Here's where you'll find the real deal:

For Crafts & Souvenirs:

- **Mercado do Bolhão:** Before it undergoes a full renovation, visit for hand-crafted souvenirs and fresh produce to feel the city's pulse.
- **Feira de Vandoma:** It's a flea market where you can hunt for vintage treasures and quirky keepsakes. Remember, the early bird catches the best deals.

Local Artistry:

- **Livraria Lello:** Famous for its literary ties, but also a spot to pick up unique Portuguese art and gifts.
- **Rua Miguel Bombarda**: This street is lined with art galleries interspersed with shops selling local artisan products.

Traditional Porto Products:

- **Claus Porto:** Pick up some beautifully packaged soaps with scents that will whisk you back to the breezy Douro riverbanks.
- **Vista Alegre:** For fine porcelain that reflects Portuguese tradition and craftsmanship.

Gourmet Souvenirs:

- **Mercado Beira-Rio:** Across the river in Vila Nova de Gaia, this market is ideal for gourmet gifts like artisanal cheeses and Douro wines.
- **A Pérola do Bolhão:** A historic store for Porto's finest dried fruits, nuts, and chocolates.

Iconic Textiles:

- **Paris em Lisboa:** Visit for high-quality Portuguese linens and textiles, a tactile memory of your travels.

Port Wine to Take Home:

- **Any of the cellars in Vila Nova de Gaia:** Not only can you taste the variety, but you can also bring a bottle (or a case) of your favorite back with you.

These stores are the essence of Porto packed into objects and flavors. Whether it's a tile, a bottle of wine, or a bar of soap, you're taking a piece of Porto's heart back home with you. Go on, find that perfect memento that'll have you toasting to your Porto memories with every glance or taste.

Key Takeaways

- We kicked off with Bonfim, where street art meets coffee art, and vintage shops double as time machines.
- Cedofeita showed us that hipster vibes and history can share a sidewalk and still get along.
- Baixa reminded us why it's the beating heart of Porto, with its buzz, its bites, and its flair for the dramatic.
- We discovered that Porto's love language is crafted in shops like Claus Porto and Mercado do Bolhão, where souvenirs are more than things; they're stories wrapped in paper.

Action Steps

- Morning Must-Do: Wake up early and snag the freshest loaf of Broa de Avintes from Padaria Ribeiro—it'll be warm, crusty, and the perfect pairing for your morning coffee.

- Treasure Hunt Tip: Arrive at Feira de Vandoma at the crack of dawn, right when the vendors are setting up, to unearth the best vintage finds before anyone else.

- Soap Souvenir Hack: Visit Claus Porto during weekday afternoons when it's less crowded, so you can leisurely sample their scents and select the perfect aromatic memento.

- Cheese and Wine: Head to Mercado Beira-Rio on a late Friday afternoon, when local vendors are more likely to offer you a taste of their products, leading to a delightful picnic by the Douro.

Conclusion

The Porto parade is over, but there is still more to see. I like to think of it as the beginning of your own great story in this city where the river and the cobblestones dance to the beat. We've not just walked through Porto; we've tasted, we've heard, we've felt, and we've lived every vibrant, whispering, and roaring corner of it.

What's tucked in your travel satchel now?

- **A Smorgasbord of Porto Eats:** You're ready to snack on every Francesinha in town, taste the subtleties of a Vinho Verde, and argue about the virtues of Bolinhos de Bacalhau like you've done it all your life.

- **A Map to the Heart of Porto:** Forget the tourist maps; you've got an insider's guide now. From the grandeur of Avenida dos Aliados to the intimate alleys of Miragaia, you're equipped to find Porto's soul beyond the azulejos.

- **Cultural Cues & Local Mores:** You know now that in Porto, a coffee break is a sacred ritual and that if you want to feel the city's pulse, you join the locals at a football match, not just any stadium.

- **Your Personal Porto Adventure:** You're set to navigate this town with the ease of a local, picking out the best spots for shopping, the coziest nooks for a midday nibble, and the perfect benches for river gazing.

So, lace up your comfiest walking shoes and charge your camera – but don't forget to look up from the lens. You're about to become an integral part of Porto's narrative, which is more than just a city. Whether it's your first time here or the return to an old flame, Porto will embrace you, surprise you, and leave you yearning for more.

But what about when the trip ends? When the suitcases are unpacked, and the photos are all that's left? Fear not, for your journey with the Portuguese language is just beginning. There's a whole world within those melodic syllables and sun-soaked words, waiting for you to dive deeper.

Don't let the adventure stop here. Our extensive resources – workbooks, audio guides, and cultural compendiums – are here to keep the flame alive. They'll be your companions as you continue to unravel the intricacies of Portuguese, the language that's as soulful as a Fado tune lingering over the Douro at dusk.

Now, off you go! It's your turn to step into its embrace, to laugh with its people, and to make memories that'll dance through your mind for years to come. Boa viagem, my friends, and may the spirit of Porto stay with you long after you've returned home!

BOOK 3

Algarve Travel Guide

Explore to Win

Introduction

Well, strap in, my sun-seeking comrade, because we are about to dive headfirst into the warm embrace of the Algarve. Each grain of sand here has its own sun-kissed narrative to tell, making this shoreline more than just a stretch of land.

Feeling the tug of wanderlust? The Algarve is the answer to that call, a haven where the cliffs are carved into postcards, and the ocean hums the tunes of ancient mariners. If you've ever felt like you're chasing the horizon, here's where you catch it.

Why the Algarve? Because here, every beach is a different chapter of the same enticing story. From the hidden coves of Lagos to the endless sands of Tavira, each wave that laps at your feet whispers secrets of discovery.

But let's be real—sometimes, the shine of popular spots dims under the shadow of tourist traps. That's where this guide swoops in. You're not just another sun hat in the crowd; you're about to become an Algarve aficionado.

Benefits? You'll sidestep the holiday hordes and unearth the Algarve's authentic charm. We're talking about:

- Dining where the locals dine, feasting on seafood that's been in the ocean just hours before.
- Discovering hidden beaches that aren't splashed across every travel brochure.
- Embracing traditions, festivals, and siestas in a way that makes you part of the Algarve's fabric, not just a spectator.

So, are you ready to let the Algarve work its magic on you? To trade the predictable for the personal? To turn postcard views into panoramic memories? Dive into this guide, and let's turn that wanderlust into a well-trodden path of your own making. Welcome to the Algarve – where the adventure begins with a single step onto its sunlit soil.

Chapter 1: Algarve - The Sun-Kissed Coast

You have arrived in the Algarve, where the sun rises over the ocean and new opportunities for exploration greet you each morning. Unspoiled beauty abounds in this land of honey-colored cliffs and blue seas. Toss aside your standard vacation routine and replace it with one as distinctive as the sand's patterns under the sun. Apply some sunscreen and get ready to soak up the sun in Portugal's sunniest spot. Let's explore the Algarve's luminous coastline, where each wave, breeze, and sunset holds a story just waiting to be told.

History and Evolution of Algarve

The Algarve was once Portugal's best-kept secret, a coastline only mentioned in passing by sailors or mentioned in poetry. A few years later, it is now the summer muse of Europe. Where did its irresistible allure come from? Let's delve into a slightly off-kilter chronology.

Back in the Day:

- **Pre-1960s:** The Algarve was all about the simple life. Fishing villages dotted the coast, and the biggest crowds were seagulls squabbling over the day's catch.
- **Chart Topper:** Picture a graph where the X-axis is time, and the Y-axis is flip-flops per square meter. Watch it spike when the 60s rolled in with their technicolor dreams of sun, sea, and sand.

The Package Holiday Boom:

- **70s and 80s:** Enter chartreuse shorts and sunburns. The Algarve becomes the 'it' spot for package holidays. Hotels mushroomed faster than you could say "Mais uma cerveja, por favor" (Another beer, please).

Golf, Glorious Golf:

- **90s Onwards:** Someone shouts "Fore!" and suddenly, the Algarve is not just beaches; it's a golf haven. If there was a leaderboard for golf courses per capita, the Algarve would be Tiger Woods.

The Luxury Lift:

- **2000s to Now:** Upscale resorts, Michelin stars, and marinas join the party. The Algarve's not just about budget breaks; it's about sipping fine wine while watching yachts bob in the marina.

Today's Treat:

- **Now:** The secret's out, and everyone's invited. The Algarve is a mosaic of cultures, with a sprinkle of history and a big dollop of natural beauty. It's got charm and chutzpah, with a side of cheeky Nando's sauce.

So, from fishing nets to jet sets, the Algarve has donned many hats (most of them sunhats). It's the coastline that turned vacationing into an art form and made the world its canvas. Want to add your own stroke of color to the Algarve's ever-expanding mural? Grab this guide, and let's paint the town – or at least, the beaches – red (sunscreen advised, of course).

Algarvian Traditions

The Algarve is not just a pretty face with sunny beaches; it's like a colorful quilt made of cultural traditions that have been passed down through the ages. Let's dive into the delightful world of Algarvian customs, as refreshing as a cool sea breeze!

Festa de São João:

Every June, the streets come alive with the Festa de São João. It's a night where everyone, from toddlers to grandmas, wields a plastic hammer playfully whacking each other on the head. Sounds quirky? Absolutely. But it's all in good fun, part of a tradition to celebrate Saint John the Baptist with bonfires, balloons, and dancing until dawn.

The Fish Markets:

In towns like Olhão and Lagos, fish markets aren't just where you pick up dinner; they're social hubs. Here, locals haggle over sea bass and gossip about their neighbors as seagulls orchestrate from above. It's a daily ritual that's been the same for generations.

The Siesta:

Oh, the sacred siesta. After a hearty lunch, don't be surprised if shops close and towns seem to take a collective nap. It's a pause that recharges the soul – and you're invited to join in. Find a shady spot and let the world slow down for a bit.

Fado:

In dimly lit tavernas, Fado, the music of longing, spills out. It's not just a genre; it's the soundtrack to the Portuguese spirit. The emotional ballads tell tales of life at sea, love lost, and the enduring strength of the human heart.

Traditional Crafts:

The Algarve's crafts are stories in tangible form. From the intricate lacework of Vila do Bispo to the pottery of Porches, these crafts aren't just souvenirs; they're pieces of heritage, handcrafted to tell the Algarve's story.

So, there you have it, a peek into the Algarve's traditions that keep the region's heart thumping strong. It's a place where the old ways dance hand-in-hand with the new, and where every tradition is an open invitation to join the celebration.

Cultural Etiquette and Norms in Algarve

1. **Greetings are Golden:** A simple "Bom dia" (Good morning) or "Boa tarde" (Good afternoon) can open doors, both literally and figuratively. Flash a smile and a greeting, and watch the warmth return tenfold.

2. **The Sacred Siesta:** Between 1 PM and 3 PM, the Algarve takes a collective breath. Shops might close, and the streets quiet down. Respect the rest, and plan your activities around it.

3. **Dining Delays:** Dinner here is a late show; restaurants rarely get buzzy before 8 PM. So, take your time, enjoy the sunset, and then dine under the stars.

4. **Beach Etiquette:** Space is a premium on the Algarve's popular beaches. Don't plonk your towel down on someone's sandy doorstep. A little space goes a long way in keeping the peace.

5. **Market Manners:** At local markets, patience is a virtue. Queue politely, and wait your turn. It's the perfect time to practice your Portuguese with a "Por favor" (Please) and "Obrigado/a" (Thank you).

6. **Coffee Culture:** Coffee here is to be savored, not rushed. Even if you order an espresso, linger over it, discuss the weather, the football, or the waves – it's not just a drink; it's a social event.

7. **Fado Respect:** If you find yourself in a Fado bar, remember it's about the performance. Keep conversations to a whisper, clapping to a hearty level post-song, and your phone tucked away.

8. **Tip with Tact:** Tipping isn't obligatory, but it's appreciated. Round up the taxi fare, leave a few euros at a nice restaurant, and watch the appreciation multiply.

If you follow these rules, you'll not only see the Algarve, but you'll also feel like you're a part of its energy. The little things that happen on trips are what make them so interesting. So go ahead and become a part of the neighborhood!

Key Takeaways

- **Festa de São João:** A joyous festival where the entire community comes together to celebrate with playful traditions and bonfires, embodying the Algarve's spirit of camaraderie.

- **Fish Market Routines:** These bustling hubs are not just for shopping but are integral to the social fabric of the Algarve, showcasing the region's deep connection with the sea.

- **Siesta Time:** The midday pause is a cherished custom, reflecting the Algarvian appreciation for a balanced pace of life.

- **Fado:** The soul-stirring melodies of Fado music, often heard in local tavernas, are a profound expression of Portuguese culture and sentiment.

- **Craftsmanship Pride:** The Algarve's traditional crafts are a window into the region's artistry, from lace to pottery, each piece tells a part of the Algarve's story.

- **Etiquette Essentials:** Understanding and respecting local customs, from greeting rituals to dining times, enhances the travel experience and fosters genuine connections with locals.

Action Steps

- **Join the Festivities:** Plan your trip around June to participate in the Festa de São João. Don't just watch; grab a plastic hammer and join in the fun.

- **Fish Market Visit:** Set your alarm for an early morning trip to the fish market. It's the best time to see it in full swing and maybe catch a fishmonger's story or two.

- **Respect the Siesta:** Use the quiet hours of the siesta for a leisurely lunch or a peaceful stroll along the beach.

- **Experience Fado:** Find a local taverna offering Fado nights. Go early to get a good seat, order a glass of local wine, and let the music transport you.

- **Support Local Artisans:** Make time to visit a pottery workshop in Porches or a lace maker in Vila do Bispo. You'll not only take home a unique souvenir but also support local traditions.

As the first part comes to a close on the sunny coast of the Algarve, we've seen a lot more than the surface. We've danced at the festas, sung along with the fado, and breathed in the salty air of the sea. Now it's time to reveal another side of this interesting area.

Next, we'll leave the busy streets behind and listen to the peaceful sounds of the Algarve's natural beauty. Get ready to be amazed by the steep cliffs, the hidden caves that only the sea knows about, and the peaceful farmland full of almond flowers. Every path goes to a view that will take your breath away, and every sunset means a fresh start.

Chapter 2: Algarve's Natural Wonders

"But Portugal has a peaceful feel about it. I sit on the terrace overlooking the vineyard there and I feel cut off from the world. You need that sort of thing."

- Cliff Richard

Hold on tight, nature lovers and people looking for peace and quiet! In the Algarve, the cliffs are the platforms, and the waves are the conductors. Chapter 2 is where we swap flip-flops for hiking boots and dive (sometimes literally) into the natural wonders that Mother Nature bragged about creating.

You will be able to explore caves that sparkle like the treasure chests of old pirate tales and roam through countryside scenes that look like they've been plucked right out of a fairy-tale illustrator's daydreams. Let's wander where the Wi-Fi is weak but the connection (to nature, that is) is off-the-charts strong.

Along the coast of the Algarve, there are beautiful beaches, steep rocks, and secluded caves. Each one has a story as old as the sea itself. Here is a full route through these beautiful natural areas:

Praia da Marinha

This beach is the poster child of Algarve postcards for a reason. With golden sands framed by limestone cliffs carved into fantastical shapes, it's a snorkeler's and sunbather's paradise. The clear waters are home to a rich marine life, perfect for when you want to swap sunbathing for underwater exploration.

How to Get There: Located near Lagoa, you can reach Praia da Marinha by car or local buses that run during the summer months. There's a parking area at the top of the cliffs with a stairway leading down to the beach.

Best Time to Visit: Come early in the morning to catch the sunrise or during the weekdays to avoid the crowds.

Benagil Caves

A marvel that looks like Mother Nature's own cathedral. The Benagil Cave, with its iconic skylight roof, is accessible only by water. Rent a kayak or join a guided boat tour to navigate your way to this natural wonder.

How to Get There: The closest town is Benagil, and from there, you can embark on a boat tour or rent a kayak. If you're an experienced swimmer, it's a short swim from Benagil Beach, but only attempt this in calm sea conditions.

Best Time to Visit: The early bird catches the worm, or in this case, the most serene view. Boat tours are less crowded in the morning.

Ponta da Piedade

There are sea pillars, bridges, and caves that make up this maze that is best seen by boat. The rocks here look like statues, and the way the sun hits them, and the water makes the stones look like an infinite array of colors.

How to Get There: Located just south of Lagos, you can drive there, and there's ample parking. From the parking area, you can walk down the stairs to the water's edge and hop on a boat tour.

Best Time to Visit: Late afternoon brings out the most dramatic light for photographs.

Praia de Odeceixe

Praia de Odeceixe is a vast crescent of sand that stretches out where the river meets the sea. The river waters lapping at one end of the beach are great for families and paddleboarders, while the ocean waves on the other end of the beach draw surfers from all over the world.

How to Get There: Nestled on the western edge of the Algarve, reach it by car or bus. During the summer, a cute train connects the town of Odeceixe to the beach.

Best Time to Visit: Morning for tranquility, afternoon for people-watching and surfing.

Ria Formosa Natural Park

Not your typical beach, but a sprawling wetland that's a haven for birdwatchers and nature lovers. With its unique barrier islands and tidal lagoons, Ria Formosa is a different world altogether.

How to Get There: Located by Faro, the park is accessible via boat tours, which you can catch from Faro, Olhão, or Tavira.

Best Time to Visit: Spring or fall, when the bird migrations turn the sky into a fluttering canvas.

Sagres Cliffs

Have you heard about the stunning cliffs of Sagres in Portugal? They're like nature's way of showing off its incredible beauty. Trust me, these cliffs will leave you in awe of the earth's raw magnificence. Come on over and take a peek. This spot right here is where the ancient folks believed the world ended and the endless sea began. It's like standing on the brink of eternity!

How to Get There: Sagres is the end of the line, so to speak. Drive or take a bus to this outpost and feel the end-of-the-world vibes.

Best Time to Visit: Sunset here is not just a daily occurrence; it's a daily spectacle.

The Algarve's natural attractions are a magnet for adventurers, explorers, and those in search of aesthetic pleasure. Each destination, from the tranquility of Marinha to the reverberation of the waves in the Benagil Caves, offers a unique opportunity to see nature's artistry up close and personal. The Algarve's beaches, cliffs, and caverns are like chapters in a novel; with each visit, you add a new page to the plot.

Algarve Adventures

You can enjoy the Algarve's beauty with your eyes and your body at the same time. This is where endorphins and adrenaline dance to the beat of the waves and the woods.

Surfing:

- **Sagres:** Here is where the rough Atlantic waves hit the shore. Sagres is the place to go whether you're a pro surfer or a beginner ready to hang ten. You can learn to ride the crests quickly at surf camps like Wavesensations.
- **Praia do Amado:** A magnet for surfers of all levels, with surf camps dotting the clifftops. It's a place where you can feel the power of the ocean beneath your board.

Hiking Trails:

- **Seven Hanging Valleys Trail:** This is the Algarve's answer to a 'walk in the park.' It's a scenic coastal path that links some of the most picturesque beaches, like Marinha and Benagil. Keep your camera ready; the views are relentless.
- **Via Algarviana:** For the trail blazers, this is a long-distance path that cuts across the Algarve's hinterland, offering a deep dive into the region's diverse landscapes.

Bird Watching:

- **Ria Formosa Natural Park:** Don your binoculars and prepare to spot everything from the flamboyant flamingo to the elusive purple swamphen. The park is a sanctuary for feathered travelers on the East Atlantic Flyway.
- **Lagoa dos Salgados:** This coastal lagoon near Albufeira is a birding hotspot. The boardwalks make it easy to explore without disturbing the wildlife.

Everything you can do in the Algarve will make your vacation more exciting. You can paddle out into the surf and feel the beat of the ocean, walk along the rocks, and enjoy the views, or watch the birds perform against a background of marshland. The Algarve is a great place to find your balance on a surfboard, your footing on a walk, or your point of view through a pair of binoculars.

Ecotourism Initiatives

With its sunny scenery and clear waters, the Algarve is more than just a vacation spot. It's also a center for ecotourism, with as many eco-friendly travel options as sunny days.

Eco-stays:

- **Eco-lodges and Agro-tourism:** Scattered throughout the Algarve are eco-lodges and farms where sustainability is a way of life. Places like the "Casa Modesta" in Olhão marry modern design with traditional practices, offering a stay that's both eco-friendly and culturally enriching.

Conservation Efforts:

- **Dolphin and Whale Watching:** Operators like "Mar Ilimitado" in Sagres offer responsible dolphin and whale watching tours, contributing to research and conservation while providing an unforgettable experience.

- **Sea Turtle Rescue:** The "Ria Formosa" coastline is home to the "Zoomarine's Rehabilitation Center," dedicated to rescuing and rehabilitating sea turtles. Visitors can learn and even participate in the release of these majestic creatures back into the wild.

Nature Tours:

- **Guided Nature Walks:** Organizations like "Algarve Walking" immerse you in the region's natural beauty on foot, minimizing impact and maximizing appreciation for the delicate ecosystems you explore.
- **Bird Watching Expeditions:** With the Algarve being a pitstop for migratory birds, tours like those offered by "A Rocha Life" provide a bird's eye view into the importance of preserving the region's natural habitats.

Sustainable Activities:

- **Organic Farm Visits:** Farms like "Quinta da Fornalha" offer hands-on experience in organic farming, inviting visitors to understand and participate in the farm-to-table cycle.
- **Eco-friendly Water Sports:** Paddleboarding and kayaking in the Algarve's many waterways provide low-impact ways to explore, with companies like "Algarve SUP" leading eco-conscious adventures.

By supporting these environmental projects, people who visit the Algarve can enjoy the area's natural beauty while also helping to keep it that way for future generations. Making memories while making a difference is what it's all about. Every journey should be as green as the hills covered in pine trees.

Responsible Traveling in Algarve

Responsible travel in the Algarve is about embracing the sun-kissed moments while ensuring the light continues to shine on its natural beauty and culture. Here's how you can tread lightly and leave only footprints in the sand:

Eat and Shop Local: Skip the chain restaurants and supermarkets. Instead, dine at family-run "tascas" where the seafood is fresh off the boat, and shop at local markets for artisanal goods and produce.

Eco-friendly Accommodations: Choose places to stay that are committed to sustainability, like "Casa Terra," where solar panels and composting are part of the everyday.

Mindful Usage: The Algarve is blessed with sunshine but can be short on rainfall. Take shorter showers, reuse towels, and turn off the tap when brushing your teeth.

Refillable Water Bottles: With refill stations dotted around, there's no need for single-use plastics. Carry a reusable bottle and enjoy the fresh Portuguese water.

Sustainable Sea Exploration: If you're diving or snorkeling, admire the sea life without touching. Remember, corals and sea creatures aren't souvenirs.

Beach Cleanliness: Enjoy the pristine beaches, but make sure to leave them that way. Pack out what you pack in and join local beach clean-ups if you can.

Eco-Mobility: Utilize the extensive network of buses and trains, rent a bike, or walk. It's healthier for you and the environment.

Embrace Traditions: Attend cultural events, learn a few phrases in Portuguese, and respect local customs. It's about connection, not just consumption.

Respectful Distance: Keep a respectful distance from any wildlife you encounter. Use binoculars instead of getting too close for that perfect shot.

By traveling responsibly in the Algarve, you're not just a visitor; you become part of the region's ongoing story of conservation and community.

Key Takeaways

- **Embrace Local Life:** Engaging with the Algarve through its local businesses, eateries, and markets enriches your travel experience and bolsters the regional economy.

- **Eco-Friendly Stays:** Opting for accommodations that prioritize sustainability helps minimize your ecological footprint and supports innovative green initiatives.

- **Water Wisdom:** Being mindful of water usage respects the Algarve's precious natural resources and contributes to regional conservation efforts.

- **Plastic Reduction:** Carrying a refillable water bottle and avoiding single-use plastics preserves the Algarve's stunning natural beauty and marine health.

- **Environmental Care:** Leaving no trace during beach visits and participating in local clean-ups makes a direct positive impact on the environment.

- **Smart Transport:** Using public transport, walking, or cycling not only reduces emissions but also offers a more immersive experience of the Algarve's landscapes.

- **Cultural Engagement:** Respecting and partaking in local traditions and customs deepens your understanding of the Algarve's cultural fabric.

Action Steps

- **Dine Local:** Make a dinner date at a small "tasca" in Tavira to taste authentic Algarvian cuisine and support family-run establishments. Try "Tasca do Xico" for a meal that feels like a hug from a Portuguese grandma.

- **Stay Green:** Book your stay at an eco-lodge like "Casa Terra" well in advance to secure your spot at one of the Algarve's sustainable sanctuaries.

- **Water Savvy:** Purchase a stylish, durable water bottle from a local market as a functional souvenir. Refill it at your accommodation before each day's adventure.

- **Beach Cleanup Participant:** Check local bulletin boards or community websites for beach cleanup events during your stay, like those organized by "Limpamare," and spend a morning giving back to the coastline you're enjoying.

- **Eco-Shopping:** Pick up a handwoven basket from a local craftsman as a shopping tote, perfect for carrying goods and reducing plastic bag usage.

As we close this chapter on the Algarve's natural wonders and responsible travel, we carry with us not just memories but a blueprint for mindful exploration. You've discovered how to walk gently upon this land, leaving only footprints in the sand and taking only memories that last a lifetime.

But our trip through the Algarve isn't over yet. Next, we'll look at the rich fabric of the area's delicious foods. In the next part, "Flavors of the Algarve," you'll be able to smell and taste food from the area that tells stories about the sea, the sun, and the land.

So, ready your palate and join me as we dive into the very essence of Algarvian culture—one delicious bite at a time. Let's turn the page to the next delicious chapter!

Chapter 3: Flavors of the Algarve

"Wet or fine, the air of Portugal has a natural happiness in it, and the people of the country should be as happy and prosperous as any people in the world."

– H.G. Wells

Chapter 3 is all about the Algarve on a plate—or in a bowl, or even on a stick. We're about to go on a culinary mission, and each dish will be a sun-drenched treat for your taste buds. There's more to this than just food. The Algarve's life story is told through a dance of spices, fish, and sweetness. Don't worry about your diet anymore; it's time to eat your way through the taste of the Algarve. Let's eat our way through history, one tasty bite at a time!

The Algarve's Seafood

The seafood in the Algarve is like a treasure box full of goodies from the Atlantic Ocean. Every meal is a chance to find new treasures. Let's go on a culinary trip along this shore full of seafood.

Cataplana de Marisco

A copper pan in the shape of a clam called a cataplana is used to cook this seafood. It's a mix of clams, prawns, and whatever else the sea had to offer that day, cooked with flavorful herbs and wine. As a result? A dish that tastes like the sound of the ocean.

Where to Try: Restaurante A Marisqueira in Albufeira is renowned for serving up a Cataplana de Marisco that'll make you want to kiss the cook.

Sardinhas Assadas

Grilled sardines are the quintessential Algarvian summer fare. Fresh off the grill, sprinkled with a dash of sea salt, and served with a wedge of lemon, they're simple, they're succulent, and they're utterly addictive.

Where to Try: Head to the sardine festival in Portimão, where the grills line the riverfront, and the air is perfumed with the scent of grilling fish.

Lagosta Suada

Steamed lobster, often enjoyed with a drizzle of buttery garlic sauce, is a celebration on a plate. It's reserved for those moments when you want to indulge, to savor, and to remember.

Where to Try: Visit Mar à Vista in Sagres, perched on a cliff with views as stunning as the lobster is flavorful.

Amêijoas à Bulhão Pato

Named after the poet Bulhão Pato, these clams are cooked in olive oil, garlic, cilantro, and white wine. It's a dish that's as much a treat for the palate as it is for the soul.

Where to Try: O Palácio in Faro offers a rendition of Amêijoas à Bulhão Pato that's worthy of sonnets.

Polvo à Lagareiro

Tender octopus baked with potatoes, drenched in olive oil, and roasted to perfection. It's as hearty as a fisherman's handshake and as satisfying as a sunset dive.

Where to Try: For a Polvo à Lagareiro that's tender enough to make you weep, book a table at A Casa do Polvo in Santa Luzia.

Doces Finos

These almond and fig-based sweets are shaped into fruits, vegetables, and fish, painted with food coloring to look almost too real to eat. They're a bite of the Algarve's sweeter side and a testament to its Moorish past.

Where to Try: Pastelaria Algarve in Faro turns these treats into edible art.

This is just a small sample of the fish and local foods that you can find in the Algarve. No matter if you're eating a simple grilled sardine or a fancy cataplana, each dish tells a story about the history, people, and sea link of the area. So, grab a fork (or just your fingers), and let's dig in!

Piri-Piri Chicken:

- **The Story:** This fiery dish traces back to Portuguese explorers who brought back piri-piri peppers from Africa. It's a blend of global journeys and local ingenuity.
- **Best Place to Try:** Restaurante Ramires in Guia claims to be the birthplace of this spicy specialty. It's a pilgrimage worth making.
- **How to Get There:** Guia is just a short drive from Albufeira. Catch a regional bus or rent a car for a quick trip inland.
- **Local Tip:** It's traditionally eaten with your hands, so dive in— just make sure you have plenty of napkins.

Seafood Rice:

- **The Story:** This dish embodies the Algarve's fishing heritage. It's a hearty, ocean-fresh meal that powered fishermen through their day.
- **Best Place to Try:** Praia da Rocha's Restaurante F - Fabrica da Ria serves a version with rice that's perfectly al dente, with seafood caught just hours before.
- **How to Get There:** Located in Portimão, it's accessible by bus or a scenic walk along the beachfront.

- **Local Tip:** Pair it with a glass of Vinho Verde for an authentic Portuguese meal experience.

Dom Rodrigos:

- **The Story:** These thread-like sweets are a nod to the Moorish influence on the Algarve, with their use of almonds and egg yolks.
- **Best Place to Try:** Pastelaria Gomba in Faro is a local favorite, where the Dom Rodrigos are as traditional as they come.
- **How to Get There:** Faro's city center is walkable, so stroll down to the marina where this pastry shop serves up the goods.
- **Local Tip:** They're quite sweet, so pair them with a bica (Portuguese espresso) to balance the flavors.

Fig and Almond Treats:

- **The Story:** Figs and almonds are staples of the Algarve's groves, and their combination in desserts reflects the region's agricultural bounty.
- **Best Place to Try:** Head to the markets in Loulé for authentic fig and almond treats made by locals, especially during the Saturday morning farmer's market.
- **How to Get There:** Loulé is a short train ride from Faro, and the market is a highlight of the town center.
- **Local Tip:** Visit in the morning when the treats are freshest, and don't be shy to ask for a sample.

These dishes, made from the sea, the land, and ages of spice-filled winds, take you back to the history of the Algarve. A meal in the Algarve is like a feast for the eyes and the ears. Come hungry for both food and stories. Remember to enjoy your meals slowly here in the Algarve; every meal is a chance to relax, not rush.

Best Spots To Relax And Enjoy a Meal

In the Algarve, wine, and food are both considered works of art. Each meal is like a scene from a tale, and the wine is like a character in its own right. Let's open some of the best places to unwind and enjoy a meal where the atmosphere is just as important as the food.

Vila Joya

The Experience: With a terrace overlooking the azure sea, Vila Joya isn't just a meal; it's a multi-sensory extravaganza. It's home to a two-Michelin-starred restaurant, where the dishes are as stunning as the ocean view.

Where to Find: Nestled in Albufeira, it's a gem waiting to be discovered along the coastal cliffs.

Local Tip: Dress to impress and book well in advance. This is fine dining with a laid-back Algarve twist.

Canico Restaurant

The Experience: Carved into the cliffs, Canico is where you dine to the soundtrack of waves. Accessible by an elevator descending through the rockface, it's both an adventure and a culinary delight.

Where to Find: Perched within the Prainha resort in Alvor, it's a hidden treasure that's worth the descent.

Local Tip: Time your dinner with the sunset for an unforgettable backdrop to your meal.

O Camilo

The Experience: Known for its fresh fish and spectacular views, O Camilo is a slice of Algarvian heaven. The seafood tastes like it jumped from the ocean to your plate.

Where to Find: Situated atop a cliff in Lagos, with panoramic views of Camilo Beach below.

Local Tip: Try their "Cataplana de Marisco" for a true taste of the sea, and don't forget to sample the local wines they have on offer.

Páteo Algarvio

The Experience: Offering a rustic and authentic Portuguese dining experience, Páteo Algarvio in Loulé is where tradition meets the taste buds.

Where to Find: In the heart of Loulé, a quaint town that's bursting with local charm.

Local Tip: Their outdoor seating is perfect for people-watching and soaking up the local atmosphere.

Adega da Marina

The Experience: This bustling spot is famous for its generous portions, convivial atmosphere, and affordable prices. It's where locals go for a no-frills, hearty meal.

Where to Find: Located on the main avenue in Lagos, it's as easy to find as it is enjoyable.

Local Tip: The grilled sardines are a must-try, and be prepared to wait for a table—it's worth it!

The Algarve has a wide range of dining options, from cozy retreats on cliffs to toasting under the stars in a town street. The landscapes are just as varied and rich as the food. Sit back and enjoy the tastes of the Algarve. One meal at a time, they will show you how to live the good life.

Key Takeaways

- **The Sea's Bounty:** We've learned that the Algarve's seafood is a treasure trove of tastes, each dish a tribute to the region's maritime heritage.

- **Spicy Piri-Piri:** A reminder that the Algarve's flavors have voyaged far and wide, with the fiery piri-piri chicken igniting our palates and stories of seafaring adventures.

- **Sweet Traditions:** The almond and fig treats told us sweet stories of the Algarve's Moorish past, wrapped in delicate shapes and colors.

- **Cataplana Experience:** This unique cooking method isn't just culinary; it's a cultural icon, symbolizing the Algarve's blend of innovation and tradition.

- **Local Wines:** From robust reds to light Vinho Verde, the Algarve's wines are as diverse and welcoming as its landscapes.

- **Dining with a View:** Places like Vila Joya and Canico don't just feed you; they feast your eyes on panoramic vistas that make every meal memorable.

Action Steps

- **Book a Table:** Make reservations ahead of time at those hot-spot restaurants like Vila Joya to ensure you get a taste of the Algarve's Michelin-starred cuisine.

- **Market Mornings:** Set out early to visit local markets like Mercado do Bolhão. Chat with the vendors, learn about the catch of the day, and pick up fresh ingredients for a beach picnic.

- **Cooking Classes:** Sign up for a traditional Portuguese cooking class to take the flavors of the Algarve home with you.

Learn how to whip up a cataplana so you can relive your holidays with every simmering stew.

- **Wine Tastings:** Don't miss out on local wineries. Schedule a few tastings, like at Quinta dos Vales, to discover your favorite Algarvian wines.

- **Sardine Festival:** If you're visiting in the summer, attend the Sardine Festival in Portimão. It's a local tradition where you can eat sardines to your heart's content and revel in the festive atmosphere.

We've feasted on the sun-kissed flavors of the Algarve, savoring everything from the zest of piri-piri to the sweetness of almond pastries. But as the sun dips below the horizon, a new side of the Algarve awakens.

Ready for the next adventure? Let's swap daylight delights for nocturnal thrills. In "Algarve After Dark," we'll uncover the vibrant nightlife that pulses through the coastal towns.

Chapter 4: Algarve After Dark

"The only thing that matters is to feel the fado. The fado is not meant to be sung; it simply happens. You feel it, you don't understand it and you don't explain it."

— Amália Rodrigues

Prepare to enter the Algarve's after-hours playground as the golden sun goes down and the curtains rise for the night. You can see the nighttime music of this coastal paradise from behind the scenes. It's where the slow beats of the day give way to the pulsing beats of bars by the water and the soft clinking of drinks at night. Get ready to dance or find the right spot on a terrace under the stars. The nights in the Algarve are a unique show, and you're invited. Let's look into the lively energy that only comes alive at night.

Nightlife Spots

For the Party Seekers:

- **NoSoloÁgua Portimão:** This beach club transforms from a relaxed day-time hangout to a vibrant nightspot. Here, you can dance beside the pool to the latest hits and occasionally catch live DJ sets.
- **Where to Find:** On the Praia da Rocha beachfront, a beacon for nightlife lovers.
- **Local Tip:** Keep an eye on their event calendar for themed parties and sunset sessions.

For the Lounge Lovers:

- **Canico:** By day, it's a restaurant carved into the cliffs, but by night, it becomes one of the Algarve's most picturesque lounges. Enjoy a cocktail as the sound of the waves sets the rhythm.

- **Where to Find:** Accessible via an elevator from the cliffs of Praia de Alvor.
- **Local Tip:** Arrive before dusk to snag the best seat for a dramatic sunset view.

For the Bar Aficionados:

- **Columbus Bar:** If cocktails are your calling, Columbus Bar in Faro is the place to be. Their mixologists craft concoctions that are both classic and inventive.
- **Where to Find:** In Faro's downtown area, perfect for a sophisticated night out.
- **Local Tip:** Try their signature cocktail made with local ingredients for a true taste of the Algarve.

For the Music Enthusiasts:

- **Club Vida:** This is Albufeira's answer to the clubbing scene, where the music doesn't stop until the early hours of the morning.
- **Where to Find:** In the heart of Albufeira, it's hard to miss with its lively atmosphere.
- **Local Tip:** Check out their themed nights for a unique experience each time you visit.

For the Casual Night Out:

- **Bon Vivant:** A rooftop terrace, live bands, and a relaxed vibe make this a must-visit in Lagos for those who enjoy a night out without the formality.
- **Where to Find:** Nestled in the bustling streets of Lagos, it's a local favorite.

- **Local Tip:** Their mojitos come highly recommended by the locals and are a refreshing nightcap under the stars.

For an Authentic Experience:

- **Fado Houses:** For a night steeped in the Portuguese tradition, visit one of the many Fado houses dotted across the Algarve, like A Tasquinha in Faro, for soulful music that tells the stories of the sea.
- **Where to Find:** Scattered across towns like Faro, Lagos, and Tavira.
- **Local Tip:** While the performances are mesmerizing, remember that it's customary to listen quietly to respect the Fado singers.

Each of these spots offers a different flavor of Algarve nightlife, from thumping bass lines to the melancholic strum of the Portuguese guitar. So, whatever your night owl preferences, the Algarve has a venue that resonates with your vibe. Just follow the moonlight.

Local Bars

Local bars in the Algarve offer a cozy retreat where conversations flow as easily as the drinks, and you're always just a toast away from making new friends. Here's where you can pull up a stool and experience the local watering holes.

The Old Taverns:

- **Bar O Castelo in Albufeira:** Tucked away in the Old Town, this bar is a relic of the past, where tales of the sea are as plentiful as the array of spirits lining the wall.
- **Local Tip:** Ask the bartender for their special "aguardente" to warm up your night.

The Chic and Trendy:

- **Rooftop Bar & Bistro at Hotel Faro:** For a more upscale experience, this spot offers stunning views of the marina and a selection of fine wines and craft cocktails.
- **Local Tip:** Get there during the golden hour for an Instagram-worthy backdrop to your evening.

The Craft Beer Aficionados:

- **Algarve Rock Brewery Tap Room in Faro:** A heaven for craft beer lovers, offering a glimpse into the region's burgeoning craft beer scene with a selection that's always fresh and innovative.
- **Local Tip:** Don't miss their tasting events where you can sample the latest brews and meet fellow beer enthusiasts.

The Sports Fans:

- **The Irish Pub in Vilamoura:** Always lively, with multiple screens showing the latest games, it's the place to root for your favorite team alongside locals and expats alike.
- **Local Tip:** Their happy hour deals are a great way to kick off an evening without breaking the bank.

The Bohemian Spirits:

- **Three Monkeys Bar in Lagos:** This bar strikes the perfect balance between a laid-back vibe and a lively atmosphere, with live music and a selection of artisanal beers.
- **Local Tip:** The jam sessions on weekends are a local highlight—bring your instrument and join in!

The Traditionalists:

- **Adega D'Alvor in Alvor:** This is a classic Portuguese "adega" offering a taste of the local lifestyle, with traditional music, tapas, and a friendly ambiance.
- **Local Tip:** Try their homemade "medronho," a traditional fruit brandy with a fiery kick.

The Wine Enthusiasts:

- **Wine Bar at Quinta dos Vales near Lagoa:** It's a vineyard, a sculpture garden, and a wine bar all in one. Here you can sip on award-winning local wines surrounded by art and nature.
- **Local Tip:** Their wine tasting paired with local cheeses is a must-do for a leisurely afternoon.

Whether you're looking to cheer with the locals over a football match or relax with a glass of wine amidst art, the Algarve's local bars offer a taste of the region's convivial spirit and laid-back lifestyle. So, find your spot, order a drink, and let the Algarve's night unfold around you.

Entertainment Options

The Algarve's entertainment scene is as diverse as its landscape, offering a myriad of options to keep you amused from dusk till dawn. Here's a rundown of entertainment options complete with localized tips to enhance your experience:

Live Music Venues:

- **Lagos Jazz Café:** Swing by for an evening where the rhythms range from sultry jazz to upbeat blues.
- **Local Tip:** Check their schedule in advance and book a table near the stage for the best acoustic experience.

Cultural Shows:

- **Centro Cultural de Lagos:** This cultural hub offers a plethora of performances from traditional Fado nights to contemporary dance.
- **Local Tip:** After the show, take a walk around the center to enjoy the various art installations.

Cinema Under the Stars:

- **Open-air Cinemas:** During the summer months, towns like Faro and Tavira host open-air cinema sessions, where you can watch international and local films under the night sky.
- **Local Tip:** Bring a cushion or a foldable chair for added comfort as seating is usually on the grass or stone benches.

Casinos:

- **Casino Vilamoura**: Try your luck at the slots or enjoy a sophisticated evening at one of the casino's live shows.
- **Local Tip:** They often have "dinner and show" deals for a full night of entertainment.

Karaoke Bars:

- **Sunset Bar in Albufeira:** Embrace your inner pop star and belt out classics at this friendly spot known for its lively karaoke nights.
- **Local Tip:** Get there early to sign up for your song; the list fills up quickly!

Themed Bars and Clubs:

- **The Pirate Bar in Praia da Rocha:** For a swashbuckling good time, enjoy themed cocktails in a bar decked out like a pirate ship.
- **Local Tip:** Don't miss the 'Pirate's Grog', their signature drink, but beware, it's as strong as it is delicious!

Family Fun:

- **Zoomarine Algarve:** By day, it's an oceanographic park with educational presentations, but it also hosts special evening events in the summer.
- **Local Tip:** Evening tickets are often discounted, and the park is less crowded.

Traditional Celebrations:

- **Medieval Fairs:** Towns like Silves turn back time with medieval fairs where the past comes to life with jousting, artisan markets, and historical reenactments.
- **Local Tip:** Dress up in medieval attire to fully immerse yourself in the experience and often enjoy discounts.

Gastronomic Festivals:

- **Seafood Festivals in Olhão:** Revel in the freshest catch at seafood festivals, where the day's best is turned into culinary masterpieces.
- **Local Tip:** Go with a group and share several dishes to taste as much variety as possible.

Tips For Enjoying Algarve's Festivals and Events

Plan Ahead:

Many festivals, especially in peak season, can draw large crowds. Research and plan your visit in advance. Book accommodations early and look into tickets for events that might require them.

Embrace Local Traditions:

Dive into the customs and participate wholeheartedly. Whether it's wearing traditional attire at a medieval fair or learning a few dance steps at a folklore festival, joining in enhances the experience.

Stay Hydrated and Protected:

The Algarve sun is no joke. Drink plenty of water and use sunscreen, even if the event is in the evening. The sun can be strong until late.

Transportation Strategy:

Festivals can mean congested roads and limited parking. Use public transport where possible, or if driving, arrive early to find parking. Some events offer special shuttle services—take advantage of these.

Respect the Venue:

Whether it's a beach party or a historical reenactment, treat the location with respect. Dispose of waste properly and be mindful of the environment.

Go Cashless When Possible:

Festivals are now increasingly offering cashless payment options for food, drinks, and merchandise. It's convenient and helps you avoid long lines at ATMs.

Capture the Memories:

Charge your devices and clear memory space for photos and videos. However, remember to live in the moment and not just behind the lens.

Local Cuisines and Crafts:

Festivals often showcase the best of local artisanal products and dishes. Don't miss out on trying something new; you may discover your new favorite food or a unique souvenir to take home.

Stay Informed:

Keep an eye on local event schedules, as they can change due to weather or other circumstances. Follow the event's social media or website for real-time updates.

Be Prepared for All Weather:

Evenings can get cool, so bring a light jacket. Likewise, a sudden rain shower can surprise you, so a small, portable umbrella can be a lifesaver.

Learn Basic Portuguese Phrases:

Knowing how to say, 'thank you', 'please', and 'excuse me' in Portuguese can go a long way in interacting with locals and showing respect for their culture.

Safety Best Practices:

Beach Safety: Always respect the flag system on beaches. A red flag means swimming is dangerous or prohibited. Also, keep an eye on your belongings when taking a dip.

Night Out: Stick to well-lit and busier streets when out at night, and always keep an eye on your drink. If you're planning to indulge, make sure you have a designated driver or use reputable taxi services.

Road Awareness: If you're driving, be cautious of narrow, winding roads, especially in the countryside. Park in designated areas to avoid fines.

Water Sports: Always use reputable operators for water sports and activities. Check that they have the necessary safety certifications and equipment.

Local Tips:

Local Emergency Number: Memorize or keep a note of the local emergency number, which is 112 in Portugal.

Pharmacy Hours: Pharmacies (farmácias) often operate on a rota system for after-hours services. Look for the green cross and check their schedules.

Sun Protection: The Algarve sun can be intense. Use a high-SPF sunscreen, and consider UV-protective swimwear for children.

Common Scams:

Time-Share Scams: Be wary of free offers or scratch cards handed out on the street that lead to high-pressure sales presentations for time-shares.

Friendly Stranger: Avoid following individuals who offer unsolicited help or tours, as they may lead you to overpriced shops or restaurants where they get a kickback.

Rental Frauds: When booking holiday rentals, use reputable websites and be cautious of deals that seem too good to be true. Always check reviews and never pay the full amount upfront via bank transfer, especially to private individuals.

Distraction Thefts: Be alert in crowded places like markets or festivals, where pickpockets might work in teams to distract you and steal your belongings.

Fake Goods: Street vendors may sell counterfeit products, from luxury brand knock-offs to fake electronics. Purchasing these items can be illegal and support unethical practices.

Key Takeaways

- **Diverse Nightlife:** From lounging in cliff-side bars to dancing in beach clubs, the Algarve offers a rich tapestry of nocturnal experiences.
- **Cultural Evenings:** The region's traditional Fado music provides an intimate glimpse into the soulful side of Portuguese culture.
- **Local Bars:** Each local bar, from the trendy rooftops to the traditional taverns, serves up its own unique slice of Algarvian life.
- **Entertainment Variety:** Whether you're into live music, cinema under the stars, or thrilling casino nights, there's something for every taste.
- **Festival Fun:** The Algarve's festivals are a vibrant celebration of local customs and gastronomy, offering immersive experiences.
- **Safety First:** Despite its laid-back reputation, it's important to stay vigilant, especially at night, to ensure a safe and enjoyable trip.
- **Scam Awareness:** Being aware of common scams like time-share traps and distraction thefts helps travelers protect themselves and their belongings.
- **Local Connection**: Engaging with locals and embracing their recommendations can lead to the most memorable and authentic experiences.

Action Steps

- **Sample the Music:** Plan an evening around a Fado performance. Look up schedules at local "casas de fado" and book in advance for an authentic musical night.

- **Bar-Hopping Strategy:** Map out a route of local bars you wish to visit. Start with a sunset view at a rooftop bar and end with a nightcap at a beachside spot.

- **Festival Participation:** Check the local events calendar and plan to attend at least one festival. Whether it's a seafood feast or a cultural parade, it's a chance to celebrate with the locals.

- **Casino Night Out:** Allocate one night for some glamor at one of the Algarve's casinos. Even if you're not a gambler, the live entertainment and atmosphere are worth experiencing.

- **Stay Safe:** Keep the number of a reliable taxi service on hand, and always share your whereabouts with someone you trust if venturing out solo.

Conclusion

Well, folks, we've zipped and zoomed through the Algarve like seagulls in a sunset sky. From secret beach picnics to twilight fado tunes that tug at the heartstrings, we've seen it all and then some. This wasn't just a tour; it was a full-blown love affair with a corner of the world that knows how to stir the soul and delight the senses.

We've feasted on ocean treasures, clinked glasses in hidden bars, and danced in the streets without a care. We've soaked up the sun, savored the spice of life (and piri-piri!), and learned that in the Algarve, every moment is a chance to celebrate. We've become part of a community that's as warm as the sand between our toes.

You're now armed with insider info to find the Algarve's best sunset spots, where the sky's ablaze and the day says goodbye with a fiery passion. You've got the lowdown on where to munch on the crunchiest almonds and the juiciest figs that tell tales of ancient trees and sunnier days.

But hey, don't let the journey stop here. There's a whole language out there waiting to be chatted, chortled, and cheerfully mangled by us brave linguists-at-heart. That's right, our "Portuguese Phrase Book" is peeking around the corner, ready to turn you into a 'pro' at 'obrigados' and 'por favors,' turning every market haggle and coffee order into a mini-adventure.

So, lace up those wanderlust shoes and keep that explorer's spark alight! The Algarve might be waving 'see ya later,' but your story's just getting its wings. Next up, you'll be ordering pastéis de nata like a boss and winning smiles from locals with a 'bom dia' so sunny it'll make the sunflowers jealous.

Get ready to chat, chuckle, and charm your way through Portugal. With a phrasebook in hand and a heart full of Algarve memories, who knows where you'll end up next? Here's to the tales yet to be told and the memories waiting in the wings. Onwards and upwards to the next chapter, my fellow globetrotters!

BOOK 4

Portuguese Phrase Book

Explore to Win

Introduction

Welcome to the gateway of genuine connection in the land of explorers and poets—welcome to the "Portuguese Phrase Book." Have you ever wondered how a few simple words can open a treasure trove of cultural riches? Or how a friendly greeting can lead to an invitation to a family dinner under the stars, where stories flow as generously as the local vinho?

Understanding and speaking a bit of Portuguese does more than just get you by. It bridges worlds, connecting you to the heart of local life. It's the difference between watching from the sidelines and dancing at the festival. It's how a market stroll turns into an impromptu language lesson with laughs and shared tales of "the big fish that got away."

The Power of "Bom Dia":

Imagine the sun-drenched streets of Porto greeting you back because you threw out a cheerful "Bom dia" to passersby. Picture the nods of approval when you thank the baker with a crisp "Obrigado" as you bite into a pastel de nata, its flaky crust crumbling to perfection.

More Than Words:

This isn't just about learning phrases; it's about weaving yourself into the fabric of Portuguese life. It's about the nods, the gestures, the expressions. It's about knowing when to cheek-kiss and when a handshake will do. It's the art of the Portuguese "chat" that can turn a simple coffee break into an afternoon of friendship.

The Benefits Unfold:

- **Cultural Respect:** Showing the effort to learn the language is a sign of respect that can turn doors into open arms.

- **Travel Richness:** Go beyond the tourist veneer and unearth the real stories, the local legends, and the grandmother's secret recipes.
- **Connections:** Language is the key to the city, the secret handshake into the community, and the first step to making lifelong friends.

So, shake off any trepidation. With each chapter, you'll gain not just phrases but insights into the Portuguese way of life. You'll learn not only how to ask for directions but also how to understand the stories told as you're guided through a village.

Whether it's your first "Olá" or you're fine-tuning your "Até logo," this phrasebook is your trusty companion. It's more than a tool; it's your passport to Portugal's soul.

Ready to start this journey? Let's open the door together. Your Portuguese adventure begins now, one "Olá" at a time. Here we go!

Chapter 1: Basic Phrases and Greetings

"Change your language and you change your thoughts."

— Karl Albrecht

Alright, let's kick off our Portuguese language adventure with some essential phrases and greetings that are your golden ticket to charming the socks off the locals. Think of this as your secret handshake into the world of pastel de nata, sunsets that blush, and conversations that flow like Douro Valley wine.

Chapter 1 is like your first dip in the ocean – exhilarating, a tad nerve-wracking, but oh-so refreshing. We're starting with the basics because every 'fado' song has a first note, and every 'azulejo' tile is part of a bigger, beautiful picture.

So, dust off your shyness and get ready to roll out some "Olá"s and "Bom dia"s with the flair of a seasoned Lisbon tram driver. By the end of this chapter, you'll be greeting, thanking, and making polite requests with the ease of a local ordering their fifth espresso of the morning. Let's turn those awkward grins into genuine connections – one cheerful "Tudo bem?" at a time. Ready? Vamos lá (let's go)!

Here's your ultimate cheat sheet to conquer the Portuguese-speaking world:

- Hello: Olá (OH-lah)
- Good morning: Bom dia (bohm DEE-ah)
- Good afternoon: Boa tarde (boh-ah TAR-deh)
- Good evening/night: Boa noite (boh-ah NOY-tuh)
- Goodbye: Adeus (ah-DEH-oosh)

- Please: Por favor (por fah-VOHR)
- Thank you (male): Obrigado (oh-bree-GAH-doh)
- Thank you (female): Obrigada (oh-bree-GAH-dah)
- You're welcome: De nada (deh NAH-dah)
- Yes: Sim (seem)
- No: Não (nowng)
- Excuse me (to get attention/pass by): Com licença (cohm lee-SEN-sah)
- Excuse me/I'm sorry: Desculpe (deh-SKOOL-peh)
- My name is...: Chamo-me... (SHAH-moh meh...)
- What's your name? (formal): Como se chama? (KOH-moh seh SHAH-mah?)
- How are you?: Como está? (KOH-moh esh-TAH?)
- I'm fine, thanks: Estou bem, obrigado/obrigada (ehs-TOH bem, oh-bree-GAH-doh/dah)
- Where is the bathroom?: Onde fica a casa de banho? (OHN-deh FEE-kah ah KAH-zah deh BAH-nyoo?)
- I don't understand: Não entendo (nowng een-TEN-doo)
- Can you speak English?: Fala inglês? (FAH-lah een-GLESH?)
- How much is this?: Quanto custa isto? (KWAN-too KOOS-tah EES-toh?)
- Cheers!: Saúde! (sow-OO-deh)
- Help!: Socorro! (soh-KOH-roo)
- Doctor: Médico/Médica (MEH-dee-koo/kah)
- I need...: Preciso de... (preh-SEE-zoo deh...)
- I like it: Gosto disto (GOHS-too DEES-toh)
- I love you: Amo-te (AH-moh-teh)
- Friend: Amigo/Amiga (ah-MEE-goo/gah)
- Beautiful: Bonito/Bonita (boh-NEE-too/tah)
- Today: Hoje (OH-zhuh)
- Tomorrow: Amanhã (ah-mah-NYAHN)
- Yesterday: Ontem (ON-tehm)
- Now: Agora (ah-GOH-rah)

- Later: Mais tarde (mah-EESH TAR-deh)
- Always: Sempre (SEHNG-preh)
- Never: Nunca (NOON-kah)
- Sometimes: Às vezes (ahsh VEZ-esh)
- Often: Muitas vezes (MOY-tahsh VEZ-esh)

Keep in mind the pronunciation hints are a guide, and the actual sounds can be best learned through listening and practice with native speakers. The 'nh' in Portuguese is similar to the 'ny' in the English word 'canyon,' and the 'lh' is akin to the 'lli' in 'million.' The 'deh' at the end of words is very soft, almost like 'dgeh' in 'badge.' With this cheat sheet in hand, you're all set to sprinkle your travels with a touch of Portuguese charm!

Informal Addressing: "Tu" vs. "Você"

Tu (too): This is the informal "you" used in Portugal, especially in Northern regions and among friends, family, or peers. It's casual, friendly, and straightforward.

- **Example:** "Como estás, tu?" - How are you?

Você (voh-SEH): While "você" is technically a third-person pronoun, it is often used in a more formal context in Brazil. However, in Portugal, "você" can sometimes be seen as overly formal or even unfriendly, so it's less commonly used in casual conversation.

- **Example:** "Como está você?" - How are you?

Formal Addressing: "O senhor" / "A senhora"

O senhor (oh seh-NYOR) / A senhora (ah seh-NYOH-rah): These terms are the formal "you" in Portuguese, equivalent to "Mr." or "Mrs./Ms." in English. They're used to show respect, especially when addressing older people, authorities, or in formal business settings.

- **Example:** "Como está o senhor?" - How are you, sir?
- **Example:** "Como está a senhora?" - How are you, ma'am?

Plural You: "Vocês"

Vocês (voh-SEHSH): In both Portugal and Brazil, "vocês" is used for the plural "you," covering both formal and informal situations. There's no distinction like "vosotros/as" in Spanish.

Example: "Vocês estão prontos?" - Are you all ready?

Note on Verb Conjugations:

The use of "tu" vs. "você" affects verb conjugations. With "tu," verbs are conjugated in the second person, while "você" takes the third-person conjugation, similar to he/she.

Pro Tip:

When in doubt, listen first. Pay attention to how others address people in different situations. It's often the safest way to gauge the appropriate level of formality.

Remember, just like the dance of the waves on the Portuguese coast, navigating between formal and informal speech is all about rhythm and feel. With practice, you'll be switching between "tu" and "senhor/senhora" as smoothly as a Fado guitarist plucks the strings.

In Portuguese, just like in any language, there are specific expressions that are commonly used to greet or bid farewell depending on the time of day. Here are some you might use throughout your day in Portugal:

Morning:

- "Bom dia" (bohm DEE-ah) — Good morning. Use this phrase from sunrise until lunchtime.
- "Uma ótima manhã" (oo-mah OH-tee-mah mahn-YAH) — Have a great morning. This is a nice way to wish someone a good start to their day.

Midday:

- "Boa tarde" (boh-ah TAR-deh) — Good afternoon. This greeting is appropriate after noon until the early evening, around 6 PM or sunset.
- "Hora do almoço!" (oh-rah doo ahl-MOH-soo) — Lunchtime! It's common to say this around midday when it's time to enjoy a leisurely Portuguese lunch.

Evening:

- "Boa noite" (boh-ah NOY-tuh) — Good evening/night. You can use this greeting when it starts to get dark and also when you're saying goodnight.
- "Uma boa noite" (oo-mah boh-ah NOY-tuh) — Have a good evening/night. This can be both a greeting or a farewell later in the evening.

Nighttime (Late):

- "Boa noite e bons sonhos" (boh-ah NOY-tuh eh bohns SON-yosh) — Goodnight and sweet dreams. This is a friendly way to say goodbye before going to bed.

General Time-Related Expressions:

- "Até logo" (ah-TEH LOH-goo) — See you later. This is a common farewell if you will see the person again later in the day.
- "Até já" (ah-TEH zhah) — See you soon. This implies that you will see the person shortly, perhaps within the same day.
- "Até amanhã" (ah-TEH ah-MAH-nyah) — See you tomorrow. Use this when you are saying goodbye and plan to see the person the next day.

Key Takeaways

- **Time-Specific Greetings:** Understanding greetings like "Bom dia" for the morning, "Boa tarde" for the afternoon, and "Boa noite" for the evening is crucial for polite and contextually appropriate communication in Portuguese.

- **Morning and Midday Phrases:** "Bom dia" and "Boa tarde" are versatile and can be used in both formal and informal settings, while "Uma ótima manhã" and "Hora do almoço!" add a bit of variety to everyday interactions.

- **Evening and Night Time Expressions:** "Boa noite" is used both as a greeting in the evening and a farewell at night, and "Boa noite e bons sonhos" is a heartfelt way to say goodnight, especially in a more personal context.

- **General Time-Related Farewells:** Phrases like "Até logo," "Até já," and "Até amanhã" are common ways to say goodbye, each indicating a different time when you expect to see the person again.

- **Cultural Nuances:** The use of these expressions can vary slightly depending on the region within the Portuguese-speaking world, highlighting the importance of cultural awareness.

- **Flexibility and Context:** Being adaptable and using the appropriate expressions based on the time of day and social setting is key to effective communication and integration into Portuguese-speaking communities.

Exercises

Multiple Choice:

1. Which greeting is typically used in the morning in Portuguese-speaking countries?
   - **a)** Boa noite
   - **b)** Boa tarde
   - **c)** Bom dia
   - **d)** Olá

2. How would you formally address someone in Portugal?
   - **a)** Tu
   - **b)** Você
   - **c)** O senhor/A senhora
   - **d)** Eles

3. Which of the following is the informal word for "you"?
   - **a)** Ele
   - **b)** Ela
   - **c)** O senhor/A senhora
   - **d)** Tu

4. What is the Portuguese word for "Thank you"?
   - **a)** Por favor
   - **b)** Obrigado/Obrigada
   - **c)** Adeus
   - **d)** Sim

5. Which phrase would you use to say goodnight to someone?
   - **a)** Olá
   - **b)** Por favor
   - **c)** Adeus
   - **d)** Boa noite

Fill in the Blanks:

1. _____ is the formal way to say "you" in Portuguese when addressing a man.
2. To say "Good afternoon," you would say _____.
3. The Portuguese word for "please" is _____.
4. When closing a conversation at night, you might say "_____."
5. If someone says "Obrigado," you could reply with "_____."

True or False:

1. "Boa noite" can be used to say both "good evening" and "goodnight."
2. The informal way to ask "How are you?" is "Como estás?"
3. "Por favor" translates to "Please."
4. "Até logo" means "See you later."
5. In Portuguese, "Não" means "Yes."

Answer Key:

Multiple Choice:

1. c) Bom dia
2. c) O senhor/A senhora
3. d) Tu
4. b) Obrigado/Obrigada
5. d) Boa noite

Fill in the Blanks:

1. O senhor
2. Boa tarde
3. Por favor
4. Boa noite
5. De nada

True or False:

1. True.
2. True, in the context of Portugal and informal settings.
3. True.
4. True.
5. False. "Não" means "No."

Chapter 2: Dining and Food

"Own only what you can always carry with you: know languages, know countries, know people. Let your memory be your travel bag."

— Aleksandr Solzhenitsyn

If you're the kind who plans your travel itinerary around meal times (who doesn't?), then get ready, because Chapter 2 is a gastronomic road trip through the heart of Portuguese flavored town. Dining in Portugal isn't just about filling the tank; it's a full-throttle adventure for your taste buds, where every dish tells a story, and every meal is a scene from a culinary epic. From the freshest seafood that leaps from the hook to your plate, to pastries so delicious they could make a grown man cry, Portuguese dining is the stuff of legend. So, grab a fork (or just your hands, we're all friends here), and let's dive fork-first into the delicious world of Portuguese dining. Ready to turn your "Hmm, what's for lunch?" into a "Wow, is this what heaven tastes like?" Let's go!

Ordering Food And Drinks In Portuguese Restaurants

Start your culinary adventure with these useful words that will make it fun to order food and drinks in Portuguese restaurants. You'll not only impress the wait staff, but you'll also make sure you get the exact Portuguese tastes you want:

- I'd like to see the menu, please. - Gostaria de ver o cardápio, por favor. (go-stah-REE-ah deh vehr o car-DAH-pee-oh, pohr fah-VOHR)

- I'll have the same as him/her. - Vou querer o mesmo que ele/ela. (voh keh-REH o MEH-zmoo keh e-lee/e-lah)
- I'm ready to order. - Estou pronto(a) para pedir. (esh-TOH prohn-too/prohn-tah PAH-rah peh-DEER)
- I'll have a steak, medium-rare. - Quero um bife, mal passado. (KEH-roo oong bee-fee, mahl pah-SAH-doo)
- Can I have a glass of red/white wine? - Posso ter um copo de vinho tinto/branco? (POH-soo tehr oong KOH-poo deh VEEN-yoo TEEN-too/BRAN-koo)
- A beer, please. - Uma cerveja, por favor. (OO-mah sehr-VEH-zhah, pohr fah-VOHR)
- Is service included? - O serviço está incluído? (o sehr-VEE-soo esh-TAH eeng-KLOO-ee-doo?)
- I have an allergy to nuts. - Tenho alergia a nozes. (TEH-nyoo ah-lehr-ZHEE-ah ah NOH-zehsh)
- What do you recommend? - O que recomenda? (o keh heh-koh-MEN-dah?)
- I'm full, thank you. - Estou satisfeito(a), obrigado(a). (ehs-TOH sah-tees-FAY-too/ah, oh-bree-GAH-doo/dah)
- That was delicious! - Estava delicioso! (ehs-TAH-vah deh-lee-SYO-zoo)
- Can I have some water, please? - Posso ter um pouco de água, por favor? (POH-soo tehr oong POO-koo deh AH-gwah, pohr fah-VOHR)
- One coffee with milk, please. - Um café com leite, por favor. (oong kah-FEH kong LAY-teh, pohr fah-VOHR)

Asking for the Bill:

- Can I have the check, please? - Posso ter a conta, por favor? (POH-soo tehr ah KOHN-tah, pohr fah-VOHR)
- Could you bring the check? - Pode trazer a conta? (POH-deh trah-ZEHR ah KOHN-tah?)

- We'd like to pay, please. - Gostaríamos de pagar, por favor. (go-stah-REE-ah-moosh deh pah-GAHR, pohr fah-VOHR)
- Separate checks, please. - Contas separadas, por favor. (KON-tahs seh-pah-RAH-dahs, pohr fah-VOHR)

Understanding Tipping Culture in Portugal:

In Portugal, like in Spain, tipping is appreciated but not mandatory. It is a way to show your gratitude for good service. Here's what you should keep in mind:

Restaurants: It's not a must to tip, but if you enjoyed your meal, consider leaving a little extra—around 5-10% is generous, and even just rounding up the bill is appreciated.

Bars and Cafés: Tipping isn't expected in casual settings. However, if you've received particularly attentive service, leaving small change is a kind gesture.

Service Charge: Always check your bill first—sometimes a service charge (serviço incluído) is already added. If that's the case, additional tipping isn't necessary.

Cash Tips: Even if paying with a card, it's preferable to leave a cash tip. It ensures that the money goes directly to your server or the staff.

Vegetarian and Vegan:

I'm a vegetarian. - Sou vegetariano/vegetariana. (soh veh-zheh-tah-ree-AH-no/ah)

I'm a vegan. - Sou vegano/vegana. (soh veh-GAH-no/ah)

Does this dish contain meat? - Este prato contém carne? (esh-TEH PRAH-too kohn-TEM KAHR-neh?)

Can I have this without cheese? - Posso ter isto sem queijo? (POH-soo teh-r eesh-TOH sehm kay-ZHOO?)

Allergies:

I'm allergic to nuts. - Sou alérgico/alérgica a frutos secos. (soh ah-LEHR-zhee-koh/ka ah FROO-toosh SEH-kosh)

I'm allergic to shellfish. - Sou alérgico/alérgica a mariscos. (soh ah-LEHR-zhee-koh/ka ah mah-REESH-kosh)

Does this contain dairy? - Isto contém lacticínios? (eesh-TOH kohn-TEM lah-tee-SEEN-yohsh?)

I can't eat gluten. - Não posso comer glúten. (nowng POH-soh koh-mehr GLOO-ten)

Preferences:

I don't like spicy food. - Não gosto de comida picante. (nowng GOHS-too deh koh-MEE-dah pee-KAHN-teh)

Can I have this without onions? - Posso ter isto sem cebolas? (POH-soo teh-r eesh-TOH sehm seh-BOH-lahsh?)

I prefer this without sugar. - Prefiro isto sem açúcar. (preh-FEE-roo eesh-TOH sehm ah-SOO-kahr)

Armed with these phrases, you can navigate Portugal's dining scene with ease and show your appreciation in a way that resonates with the locals. Enjoy your meals, and when in doubt, a smile and a "Obrigado/a" will always be welcome!

Here's a tasty list of typical Portuguese dishes and their correct pronunciations to help you order like a local:

- Bacalhau à Brás (bah-kah-LYOW ah BRAHZ) - A delightful mix of shredded salt cod, onions, and straw fries, all bound with scrambled eggs.

- Caldo Verde (KAHL-doo VEHR-d(eh)) - A comforting green soup made with potatoes, collard greens, and slices of chorizo.

- Feijoada à Transmontana (fay-ZHWAH-dah ah trahnz-mon-TAH-nah) - A hearty bean stew with various types of meat, often enjoyed in the colder months.

- Francesinha (fran-seh-ZEEN-yah) - Porto's famous sandwich, smothered in cheese and a thick tomato and beer sauce, often served with fries.

- Pastéis de Nata (pahsh-TAYSH deh NAH-tah) - The iconic Portuguese custard tarts, best enjoyed warm with a sprinkle of cinnamon and powdered sugar.

- Polvo à Lagareiro (POHL-voo ah lah-gah-RAY-roo) - Tender octopus served with roasted potatoes and drizzled with olive oil.

- Cozido à Portuguesa (koh-ZEE-doo ah poor-too-GAY-zah) - A traditional Portuguese stew made with a variety of meats, sausages, and vegetables.

- Arroz de Marisco (ah-ROZ deh mah-REE-skoo) - A flavorful seafood rice dish, akin to a paella, brimming with fresh shellfish.

- Bifanas (bee-FAH-nahsh) - Thinly sliced pork steak sandwiches seasoned with garlic and spices, often served at snack bars.

- Alheira (ah-LAY-rah) - A flavorful sausage typically made from a mix of meats (excluding pork) and bread, traditionally served with fried potatoes and a fried egg.

- Sardinhas Assadas (sar-DEEN-yahsh ah-SAH-dahsh) - Grilled sardines, a summer favorite, especially during the festival of St. Anthony.

- Açorda (ah-SOR-dah) - A simple, rustic dish made with bread, garlic, coriander, olive oil, water, and poached eggs, sometimes with shrimp or other seafood.

Key Takeaways

- **Diversity of Flavors:** Portuguese cuisine offers a wide range of flavors, from the sea's bounty in dishes like "Bacalhau à Brás" to the rich, meaty "Feijoada à Transmontana."

- **Iconic Dishes:** Certain dishes like "Pastéis de Nata" and "Francesinha" are not just food items but cultural icons, synonymous with Portuguese culinary pride.

- **Regional Specialties:** Each region in Portugal has its signature dishes, such as "Polvo à Lagareiro" from the coastal areas, highlighting the importance of locality in Portuguese cooking.

- **Seasonal Eating:** Many Portuguese dishes are tied to specific seasons or festivals, like "Sardinhas Assadas" during the summer festivals.

- **Rustic and Hearty:** Meals like "Cozido à Portuguesa" and "Açorda" demonstrate the rustic, hearty nature of traditional Portuguese meals, often designed to feed a family or community.

- **Importance of Freshness:** The emphasis on fresh, high-quality ingredients is paramount in dishes like "Arroz de Marisco," where the seafood's freshness is the star.

- **Portuguese Bread:** Bread is an essential element of Portuguese dining, often used creatively in dishes such as "Alheira" and "Açorda."

- **Tasting Tradition:** Dishes such as "Bifanas" are not just quick bites but a taste of Portuguese history and tradition, often enjoyed in local tasquinhas (taverns).

Exercises

Multiple Choice

1. How would you ask for a typical Portuguese custard tart in a cafe?
   a) Posso ter um pastel de nata, por favor?
   b) Uma cerveja, por favor.
   c) Onde está o banheiro?
   d) Quero uma sopa, por favor.

2. Which phrase would you use to indicate you want your steak well-done?
   a) Mal passado.
   b) Bem passado.
   c) Não quero bife.
   d) Sem carne, por favor.

3. If you want to order seafood rice, you would ask for:
   a) Arroz de pato.
   b) Arroz de marisco.
   c) Bacalhau à Brás.
   d) Feijoada.

4. How do you say "beer" in Portuguese?
   a) Vinho.
   b) Água.
   c) Cerveja.
   d) Sumo.

5. To express that a dish was delicious, you would say:
   a) Estava horrível.
   b) Estava delicioso.
   c) Não gostei.
   d) Estou cheio.

Fill in the Blanks

1. If you want to say you are vegetarian, you would say "Sou _____." in Portuguese.
2. To enjoy a coffee with milk in Lisbon, you'd order "Um _____ com leite, por favor."
3. When craving Francesinha, you might say, "Quero experimentar a _____, por favor."
4. For a no meat preference, you could specify "Sem _____, por favor."
5. To compliment the chef on a great meal, you might say "O jantar estava _____, obrigado."

True or False

1. "Francesinha" is a light vegetarian dish.
2. "Polvo à Lagareiro" is a popular way to prepare octopus.
3. "Bifanas" are traditional Portuguese sandwiches.
4. "Cozido à Portuguesa" is a seafood dish.
5. Tipping is expected and should be 10-15% in Portugal.

Answer Key:

Multiple Choice:

1. a) Posso ter um pastel de nata, por favor?
2. b) Bem passado.
3. b) Arroz de marisco.
4. c) Cerveja.
5. b) Estava delicioso.

Fill in the Blanks:

1. vegetariano/vegetariana
2. café
3. Francesinha
4. carne
5. excelente

True or False:

1. False. Francesinha is a meat-heavy dish.
2. True.
3. True.
4. False. It's a stew of various meats and vegetables.
5. False. Tipping is appreciated but not mandatory in Portugal, and when given, it's usually around 5-10%.

Chapter 3: Directions and Transportation

"If you talk to a man in a language he understands, that goes to his head. If you talk to him in his own language, that goes to his heart."

– Nelson Mandela

Alrighty, buckle up for Chapter 3, where we'll transform you into a Portugal street-navigating superstar! Get ready to conquer those twisty-turny roads and soak in the breathtaking views like a boss. Wave goodbye to the classic tourist look of wide eyes and a map in your hand, and say hello to confident strides and savvy travel banter!

Asking For and Understanding Directions in Portuguese:

- Where is...?: Onde fica...? (OHN-deh FEE-kah?)
- Can you help me?: Pode me ajudar? (POH-deh meh ah-zhoo-DAR?)
- I'm lost.: Estou perdido/a. (ehs-TOH-ooh pehr-DEE-doo/dah)
- How do I get to...?: Como chego a...? (KOH-moo SHEH-goo ah?)
- Go straight.: Siga em frente. (SEE-gah ehn FREN-teh)
- Turn left.: Vire à esquerda. (VEE-reh ah esh-KEHR-dah)
- Turn right.: Vire à direita. (VEE-reh ah dee-RAY-tah)
- At the corner.: Na esquina. (nah esh-KEE-nah)
- At the traffic light.: No semáforo. (noh seh-MAH-foh-roh)
- Take the first/second/third exit.: Pegue a primeira/segunda/terceira saída. (PEH-goo eh pree-MAY-rah/seh-GOON-dah/tehr-SAY-rah sa-EE-dah)

- Is it far from here?: Fica longe daqui? (FEE-kah LOHN-geh dah-KEE?)
- Is it close by?: Fica perto? (FEE-kah PEHR-too?)
- Can I walk there?: Posso ir a pé? (POH-soo eer ah peh?)
- Where is the bus station?: Onde fica a estação de ônibus? (OHN-deh FEE-kah ah es-tah-SOUNG deh OH-nee-boos?)

These phrases will help you navigate the charming streets of Portugal, whether you're in a bustling city or a quaint village. Remember, a little politeness goes a long way, so starting with a "Desculpe" (Excuse me) or "Por favor" (Please) can make your interactions smoother. And don't worry if you have to ask multiple times – the Portuguese are known for their friendly and helpful nature. Boa sorte! (Good luck!)

Phrases Related to Public Transportation

What time does the bus/train leave?

- A que horas parte o autocarro/comboio? (ah keh OH-rahsh PAR-teh o aw-toh-KAR-roh/kom-BOY-oh?)

What time does the bus/train arrive?

- A que horas chega o autocarro/comboio? (ah keh OH-rahsh SHEH-gah o aw-toh-KAR-roh/kom-BOY-oh?)

How much is a ticket to...?

- Quanto custa um bilhete para...? (KWAN-too KOOS-tah oong bee-LYEH-teh PAH-rah...?)

Does this bus/train stop at...?

- Este autocarro/comboio para em...? (ESH-teh aw-toh-KAR-roh/kom-BOY-oh PAH-rah ehn...?)

Where does this bus/train go?

- Para onde vai este autocarro/comboio? (PAH-rah OHN-deh vai ESH-teh aw-toh-KAR-roh/kom-BOY-oh?)

Is this seat taken?

- Este lugar está ocupado? (ESH-teh loo-GAR esh-TAH oh-koo-PAH-doo?)

Can you tell me when we get to...?

- Pode dizer-me quando chegarmos a...? (POH-deh DEE-zehr me KWAHN-doo sheh-GAR-moosh ah...?)

I would like to buy a [single/return] ticket.

- Gostaria de comprar um bilhete [de ida/de ida e volta]. (go-STAH-ree-ah deh kom-PRAR oong bee-LYEH-teh [deh EE-dah/deh EE-dah ee VOHL-tah])

When is the next bus/train to...?

- Quando é o próximo autocarro/comboio para...? (KWAHN-doo eh o PROKS-ee-moo aw-toh-KAR-roh/kom-BOY-oh PAH-rah...?)

Where is the bus/train station?

- Onde fica a estação de autocarro/comboio? (OHN-deh FEE-kah ah es-tah-SOUNG deh aw-toh-KAR-roh/kom-BOY-oh?)

I need to transfer at...

- Preciso de fazer transbordo em... (preh-SEE-zoo deh FAH-zehr trahns-BOR-doo ehn...)

Does this bus/train have a connection to...?

- Este autocarro/comboio tem ligação para...? (ESH-teh aw-toh-KAR-roh/kom-BOY-oh tehn lee-GA-soun PAH-rah...?)

I missed my stop.

- Perdi a minha paragem. (PEHR-dee ah MEE-nyah PAH-rah-zhehm)

Key Takeaways

- Knowing how to ask for bus or train schedules is essential – "A que horas parte/chega...?" helps you plan your journey.

- Understanding ticket prices and asking "Quanto custa um bilhete para...?" ensures you stay within your travel budget.

- Confirming your route with "Este autocarro/comboio para em...?" avoids any unnecessary detours.

- "Para onde vai este autocarro/comboio?" helps you to make sure you're on the right path to your intended destination.

- Inquiring if a seat is available with "Este lugar está ocupado?" is a polite way to find seating.

- Asking the driver or fellow passengers to inform you of your stop, "Pode dizer-me quando chegarmos a...?" can prevent you from missing it.

- Being able to request the correct type of ticket – single or return – with "Gostaria de comprar um bilhete de ida/de ida e volta" is crucial.

- "Quando é o próximo autocarro/comboio para...?" Helps you catch the next available ride without long waits.

- Knowing how to ask for the station's location – "Onde fica a estação de autocarro/comboio?" – is fundamental when navigating Portuguese cities.

- If you need to change lines, "Preciso de fazer transbordo em..." is useful for smooth transitions.

Exercises

Multiple Choice

1. How would you ask for directions to the train station in Portuguese?
   - **a)** Onde está o banheiro?
   - **b)** Onde fica a estação de comboio?
   - **c)** Quanto custa o comboio?
   - **d)** Tem um mapa?

2. Which phrase would you use to ask for a taxi?
   - **a)** Quero um autocarro
   - **b)** Quero um comboio
   - **c)** Quero um táxi
   - **d)** Quero uma bicicleta

3. How would you ask for a ticket to Porto?
   - **a)** Um bilhete para o Porto, por favor
   - **b)** Uma mesa para o Porto
   - **c)** Um café para o Porto
   - **d)** Um carro para o Porto

4. What is the Portuguese phrase for "one-way ticket"?
   - **a)** Volta completa
   - **b)** Bilhete de ida
   - **c)** Dois bilhetes
   - **d)** Bilhete de ida e volta

5. How would you say "stop here, please" to a bus driver?
   - **a)** Pare aqui, por favor
   - **b)** Siga aqui, por favor
   - **c)** Vire aqui, por favor
   - **d)** Continue aqui, por favor

Fill in the Blanks

1. _____ means "Where is the bathroom?" in Portuguese.

2. To ask for "the next train," you would say _____.
3. The Portuguese phrase for "I would like to rent a car" is _____.
4. When asking for a timetable, you might say "_____".
5. If you want to ask "How much is the fare?" you would say "_____".

True or False

1. "Autocarro" means "car."
2. "Quando parte o próximo comboio?" Means "When does the next train leave?"
3. "Voo" translates to "train."
4. "Um bilhete de ida" means "a one-way ticket."
5. "Aberto" is used to describe an open road.

Answer Key

Multiple Choice:

1. b) Onde fica a estação de comboio?
2. c) Quero um táxi
3. a) Um bilhete para o Porto, por favor
4. b) Bilhete de ida
5. a) Pare aqui, por favor

Fill in the Blanks:

1. Onde está o banheiro?
2. Quando parte o próximo comboio?
3. Gostaria de alugar um carro
4. Pode dar-me o horário?
5. Quanto é a tarifa?

True or False:

1. False. It means "bus."
2. True.
3. False. It means "flight."
4. True.
5. False. "Aberto" means "open," and "estrada" is the word for "road."

Chapter 4: Accommodations and Shopping

"A different language is a different vision of life."

— Federico Fellini

This is where the rubber meets the road—or should we say, where the credit card meets the shopping spree? Here, you'll learn to book a bed as soft as a cloud and find deals so good they'll make your wallet weep with joy. By the end, you'll be tossing out "Quanto custa isso?" with the swagger of a local and the smarts of a seasoned haggler. Ready to shop 'til you drop and sleep like a log afterward? Let's roll!

Booking a Hotel Room and Asking For Specific Accommodations in Portuguese:

- I'd like to book a room - Gostaria de reservar um quarto. (go-STAH-ree-ah deh heh-zeh-VAHR oong KWAR-too)
- Do you have any rooms available? - Têm quartos disponíveis? (tain KWAR-toos deesh-pon-EE-vehsh?)
- I need a room for two nights - Preciso de um quarto para duas noites. (preh-SEE-zoo deh oong KWAR-too PAH-rah DWASH NOY-tsh)
- Single room - Quarto individual. (KWAR-too een-dee-vee-JOO-al)
- Double room - Quarto duplo. (KWAR-too DOO-ploo)
- Suite - Suíte. (SWEE-tche)
- With a sea view - Com vista para o mar. (kong VEESH-tah PAH-rah o mah)

- With a private bathroom - Com banheiro privado. (kong bah-NYEY-roo pree-VAH-doo)
- Is breakfast included? - O café da manhã está incluído? (o kah-FEH dah MAH-nyah esh-TAH een-kloo-EE-doo?)
- Can I have a late checkout? - Posso fazer o checkout mais tarde? (POH-soo FAH-zehr o check-OWT MAISH TAR-jee?)
- I need a room with WiFi - Preciso de um quarto com WiFi. (preh-SEE-zoo deh oong KWAR-too kong WEE-fee)
- Do you allow pets? - Permitem animais de estimação? (pehr-MEE-tehn ah-nee-MAH-eej deh esh-tee-ma-SOUNG?)
- Is there a gym? - Tem ginásio? (tain zhee-NAH-syoo?)
- I'd like to cancel my reservation - Gostaria de cancelar a minha reserva. (go-STAH-ree-ah deh kahn-seh-LAHR ah MEE-nyah heh-ZEHR-vah)
- Where is the elevator? - Onde fica o elevador? (OHN-gee FEE-kah o el-eh-va-DOR?)
- Do you have parking? - Têm estacionamento? (tain es-tah-syoh-nah-MEN-too?)

Shopping Phrases in Portuguese:

- How much does this cost? - Quanto custa isto? (KWAN-too KOOS-tah EESH-too?)
- I'm looking for a souvenir - Estou à procura de uma lembrança. (ESH-toh ah proo-KOO-rah deh OO-mah lehm-BRAN-sah)
- Do you have this in another size? - Têm isto em outro tamanho? (tain EESH-too ehn OW-troo tah-MAN-yoo?)
- Can I try this on? - Posso experimentar isto? (POH-soo ehs-peh-ree-men-TAHR EESH-too?)
- Where are the fitting rooms? - Onde estão os provadores? (OHN-jee esh-TOUN os proh-va-DOH-resh?)
- I'll take this - Vou levar isto. (voh LEH-var EESH-too)
- Do you accept credit cards? - Aceitam cartões de crédito? (ah-SAY-tahm kar-TOUNSH deh KREH-dee-too?)

- I need a gift - Preciso de um presente. (preh-SEE-zoo deh oong preh-ZEN-chee)
- Do you have a sale? - Está em promoção? (esh-TAH ehn proh-mo-SOUN?)
- I'm just looking, thank you - Só estou olhando, obrigado. (soh ESH-too oh-LAHN-doo, oh-bree-GAH-doo)
- Where can I find souvenirs? - Onde posso encontrar lembranças? (OHN-jee POH-soo ehn-kohn-TRAHR lehm-BRAN-sahsh?)
- Can you wrap this as a gift? - Pode embrulhar isto como presente? (POH-jee ehm-broo-LYAHR EESH-too KOH-moo preh-ZEN-chee?)
- Do you have this in another color? - Têm isto em outra cor? (tain EESH-too ehn OW-trah kor?)
- Is this handmade? - Isto é feito à mão? (EESH-too eh FAY-too ah moun?)
- Can I return or exchange this? - Posso devolver ou trocar isto? (POH-soo deh-VOL-ver oo tro-KAHR EESH-too?)

Bargaining and Understanding Currency in Portuguese:

Bargaining Phrases:
- Há desconto? (ah deh-SKON-too?) — Is there a discount?
- Pode fazer um preço melhor? (POH-deh FAH-zer oong PREH-soo meh-LHOR?) — Can you give me a better price?
- Está muito caro. (esh-TAH MOO-ee-too KAHR-oo) — It's too expensive.
- Posso pagar... (POH-soo pah-GAHR...) — I can pay...

- Qual é o menor preço que pode fazer? (kwahl eh o meh-NOR PREH-soo keh POH-deh FAH-zer?) — What's the lowest price you can offer?
- Eu levo por... (e-oo LEH-voo por...) — I will take it for...

Understanding Currency:

- Qual é a taxa de câmbio? (kwahl eh ah TAH-shah deh KAHM-byoo?) — What is the exchange rate?
- Onde posso trocar dinheiro? (ON-deh POH-soo troh-KAHR dee-NAY-roo?) — Where can I exchange money?
- Posso pagar em euros? (POH-soo pah-GAHR ehn EH-oo-roosh?) — Can I pay in euros?
- Quanto é isto em euros? (KWAN-too eh EESH-too ehn EH-oo-roosh?) — How much is this in euros?
- Aceitam moeda estrangeira? (ah-SAY-tam MOH-ay-dah ehs-trahn-JAY-rah?) — Do you accept foreign currency?
- Há alguma taxa por usar cartão de crédito? (ah ahl-GOO-mah TAH-shah por OO-zahr kar-TOUN deh KREH-dee-too?) — Is there a fee for using a credit card?

Asking For Help and Information:

In Stores:

- Com licença, pode me ajudar? (kong lee-SEN-sah, POH-deh meh ah-zhoo-DAR?) — Excuse me, can you help me?
- Onde posso encontrar...? (ON-deh POH-soo ehn-kohn-TRAHR...?) — Where can I find...?
- Tem isto noutra tamanho/cor? (tain EESH-too NOH-trah tah-MAN-yoo/kor?) — Do you have this in another size/color?
- Posso experimentar isto? (POH-soo ehs-peh-ree-men-TAR EESH-too?) — Can I try this on?

- Quanto custa isto? (KWAN-too KOOS-tah EESH-too?) — How much does this cost?
- Onde está o provador? (ON-deh esh-TAH o proh-va-DOR?) — Where is the fitting room?

In Hotels:

- Posso ter o meu quarto limpo? (POH-soo tair o may-oo KWAR-too LEEN-poo?) — Can I have my room cleaned?
- Pode chamar um táxi para mim? (POH-deh SHA-mar oong TAHK-shee PAH-rah meeng?) — Can you call a taxi for me?
- A que horas é o café da manhã? (ah keh OH-rash eh o kah-FEH dah MAH-nyah?) — What time is breakfast served?
- Posso fazer o checkout mais tarde? (POH-soo FAH-zer o check-OWT MAISH TAR-deh?) — Can I have a late checkout?
- Há Wi-Fi no quarto? (ah WEE-fee noo KWAR-too?) — Is there Wi-Fi in the room?
- Tenho uma reserva em nome de... (TEN-yoo oong ah heh-ZEHR-vah ehn NOH-mee deh...) — I have a reservation under the name...

Key Takeaways

- Bargaining is an Art: Master a few key phrases like "Há desconto?" to negotiate prices and secure deals that make both you and the vendor smile.

- Understanding the Currency: Get a handle on the euro with "Qual é a taxa de câmbio?" and learn where to exchange money to avoid being stuck with a wallet full of the wrong currency.

- Hotel Savvy: Booking the perfect room is about the right questions – from "Posso ter o meu quarto limpo?" for cleanliness to "Há Wi-Fi no quarto?" for staying connected.

- Shopping Smarts: Dive into local commerce with essential queries such as "Quanto custa isto?" and "Onde está o provador?" to ensure you're getting exactly what you want.

- Credit Card Know-How: Always ask "Há alguma taxa por usar cartão de crédito?" to avoid unexpected fees when paying with plastic.

- Gift Wrapping Service: Don't forget to ask "Pode embrulhar isto como presente?" to make your souvenirs gift-ready on the go.

- Room Specifications: Specify your needs with "Gostaria de um quarto com vista para o mar" to enhance your stay with picturesque views.

- Pet-Friendly Options: If traveling with furry friends, "Permitem animais de estimação?" ensures your companions are welcome.

- Cultural Insight: Immersing yourself in the local shopping culture is not just about purchases; it's about interaction and cultural exchange.

- Local Assistance: "Com licença, pode me ajudar?" is your go-to phrase for seeking help, proving that politeness opens more doors.

Exercises

Multiple Choice

1. What Portuguese phrase would you use to ask for a room with a view?
   - a) Posso ter um quarto sem vista?
   - b) Posso ter uma vista?
   - c) Gostaria de um quarto com vista.
   - d) Não quero um quarto com vista.

2. How would you ask if breakfast is included in your hotel stay in Portuguese?
   - a) O café da manhã está incluído?
   - b) O jantar está incluído?
   - c) Onde está o café da manhã?
   - d) Posso tomar o café da manhã?

3. Which phrase would you use to ask for the price in a Portuguese store?
   - a) Quanto custa isso?
   - b) Quanto é isso?
   - c) Isso custa quanto?
   - d) All of the above.

4. If you wanted to bargain for a lower price, what could you say?
   - a) Isso é muito caro.
   - b) Não posso pagar isso.
   - c) Pode baixar o preço?
   - d) Pode me dar de graça?

5. When shopping and you need a different size, you would ask:
   - a) Tem um tamanho diferente?
   - b) Tem outra cor?
   - c) Onde está o provador?
   - d) Isso é feito à mão?

Fill in the Blanks

1. When looking for a fitting room, you ask "_____ está o provador?"
2. To say "I would like to book a room," in Portuguese, you say "_____ reservar um quarto."
3. If you want to know if pets are allowed at the hotel, you would ask "_____ animais de estimação?"
4. To find out if you can pay by card, you might ask "_____ cartões de crédito?"
5. To request your room to be cleaned, say "_____ ter o meu quarto limpo?"

True or False

1. "Posso pagar com cartão?" means "Can I pay with a card?"
2. "Quarto duplo" refers to a double room.
3. "Aceitam dólares?" is asking if dollars are accepted.
4. "Onde posso trocar dinheiro?" Means "Where can I exchange money?"
5. "Pode me dar um desconto?" is asking for a discount.

Answer Key

Multiple Choice:

1. c) Gostaria de um quarto com vista.
2. a) O café da manhã está incluído?
3. d) All of the above.
4. c) Pode baixar o preço?
5. a) Tem um tamanho diferente?

Fill in the Blanks:

1. Onde
2. Gostaria de
3. Permitem
4. Aceitam
5. Posso

True or False:

1. True.
2. True.
3. True. (But it's always best to check if the specific place you're at accepts foreign currency.)
4. True.
5. True.

Conclusion

And there we have it, your very own passport to Portugal's language landscape, tucked snugly between the folds of this book. You've dipped your toes into the refreshing waters of Portuguese phrases, and now the entire ocean beckons you to dive in. It's more than words; it's an invitation to a feast of culture and connection.

Throughout these pages, you've gathered the linguistic tools not just to survive, but to thrive. From the 'Bom dia' that brightens a local's morning to the 'Obrigado' that warms a shopkeeper's heart, every phrase you've learned is a bridge to a new friendship, a new story, a new memory.

Yet, the journey doesn't end when you reach the back cover. It's just the beginning:

- Practice Makes Perfect: Chat up the café barista, exchange pleasantries with the street vendor, and navigate the cobblestone alleys with confidence. Every interaction is a step towards fluency.

- Cultural Immersion: Let the language lead you to hidden spots off the beaten path, to experiences that tourists rarely glimpse, and to moments that you'll tuck away in your heart forever.

- Share and Grow: Become an active member of the Portuguese-speaking community. Share your experiences, your bloopers, and your victories. Every shared story knits the world a little closer together.

As you set out on your travels, let this book be your trusty companion. It's the key that unlocks the full, rich experience of Portugal. You'll discover that every 'Por favor' opens more than just doors; it opens hearts, and every 'Adeus' is not a goodbye, but an invitation to return.

So, go ahead, step out with a suitcase full of phrases and a heart full of anticipation. Portugal is not just a place to see, but a place to feel, and now, a place to speak about in its own tongue.

Boa viagem! May your travels be as delightful as the language you now hold in your hands. And remember, the end of this book is only the start of your conversation with Portugal.

Book Description

In this definitive travel series, you will see Portugal like never before. Whether you're a culture enthusiast, a history buff, or a culinary connoisseur, this collection will transform your Portuguese escapade into a tapestry of vibrant experiences and vivid memories.

Are you yearning for an authentic Portuguese adventure beyond the typical tourist traps?

Have other travel guides left you yearning for more depth and less fluff?

Do you desire to weave through the cultural fabric of Portugal and emerge with a profound connection to its land and people?

If you're nodding along, then you've struck gold with this collection.

This series is more than a travel guide because of the way it addresses language difficulties and cultural sensitivities head-on. Fado's stirring rhythms in Lisbon, Porto's romantic wine cellars, and the Algarve's sun-kissed beaches await you on your adventure, each offering something unique and exciting.

In the **Portugal Travel Series**, you'll find:

- The allure of Lisbon, with insider tips to local hotspots and hidden gems that promise an authentic slice of city life.
- A love letter to Porto, weaving through its historic streets and riverside charm, all while guiding you to the must-visit places that define the city's soul.
- The Algarve's best-kept secrets, from cliffside wonders to azure waters, ensure your seaside retreat is nothing short of magical.
- The ultimate Portuguese phrase book, arming you with the linguistic prowess to charm locals and navigate the country with ease and flair.

Leave behind the fears of misadventure as this series ensures you:

- Walk the cobbled streets with the confidence of a local, knowing you're privy to the same secrets that they cherish.
- Savor the gastronomic delights of Portugal, understanding the stories behind every dish and the proper etiquette to enjoy them.
- Fall in love with the Portuguese way of life, embracing the customs, celebrations, and daily rhythms that make Portugal a place of endless discovery.

Don't just visit Portugal—immerse yourself in it. Let the Portugal Travel Series be your companion as you step beyond the pages and into the vivid reality of this stunning country.

Ready to transform your Portuguese travels from ordinary to extraordinary? Then, **add this series to your cart** and set sail for an adventure that promises to be as captivating as the land of explorers and poets itself!

Made in the USA
Las Vegas, NV
21 September 2024

95601487R00105